T0318251

Arab American Children with Disabilities

Despite a proliferation of special education literature on racial minorities over the past three decades, research and writing on Arab American children with disabilities remain remarkably sparse. This book fills that gap by promoting culturally appropriate services for Arab American children with disabilities. Special education and service providers in the U.S.—including school psychologists, rehabilitation counselors, and social workers—are increasingly likely to work with Arab Americans with disabilities. By focusing on this marginalized minority population, Al Khatib provides much-needed context and direction for service providers and researchers working with the Arab American community. Offering an overview of special education and the rights guaranteed under the Individuals with Disabilities Education Act (IDEA), this book also helps Arab American families understand the special education process and advocate for their children.

Jamal M. Al Khatib is Professor of Special Education at the University of Jordan, Jordan.

Arab American Children with Disabilities
Considerations for Teachers and Service Providers

Jamal M. Al Khatib

Routledge
Taylor & Francis Group

NEW YORK AND LONDON

First published 2017
by Routledge
605 Third Avenue, New York, NY 10017

and by Routledge
2 Park Square, Milton Park, Abingdon, Oxon, OX14 4RN

Routledge is an imprint of the Taylor & Francis Group, an informa business

First issued in paperback 2021

Library of Congress Cataloging-in-Publication Data
A catalog record for this book has been requested

Typeset in Times New Roman
by Apex CoVantage, LLC

ISBN 13: 978-0-367-54788-2 (pbk)
ISBN 13: 978-1-138-20706-6 (hbk)
ISBN 13: 978-1-315-46329-2 (ebk)

DOI: 10.4324/9781315463292

Contents

Preface   vii

1   Arab Americans   1

2   Disability Among Arab Americans   24

3   Arab American Children with Disabilities and Special
    Education in the United States   61

4   Considerations in Working with Arab American
    Children with Disabilities   74

5   Conclusions   97

    Index   105

Preface

While working on my doctorate in special education at the Ohio State University in the early 1980s, I was asked by one of my respected professors, who was interested in multicultural special education, to write a paper about disability among Americans of Arab descent. He told me then that the Arab American community was growing and that no attention was being paid to its unique needs and challenges. I wrote a paper, but the journal I approached asked for extensive revisions. Because I was very busy working on my dissertation, I put that paper aside. The manuscript was eventually lost, and my research priorities shifted after graduating and accepting a position at the University of Jordan. Arab Americans were not among my priorities; nevertheless, I occasionally read abstracts of articles about this population but never came across a single journal article about Arab Americans and disability.

When I became a resident of the United States a little more than 5 years ago, disability among Arab Americans captured my interest; and I began tirelessly searching the literature on disability among members of this community. I found that not one journal article addressing Arab Americans and special education in the United States had been published. Thus, I was determined to write this book, hoping that it will shed light on this forgotten subminority of the most marginalized and stereotyped minority in the United States. More importantly, I hope this book will serve as a roadmap for future empirical research and improved practices with this segment of the American population. The long-term benefits for both Arab Americans with disabilities as well as for schools, I think, are quite obvious for policy makers, researchers, and practitioners.

What also piqued my interest in the last 5 years is what I may call the "I know someone" response. Whenever I replied "special education" to both experts' and laypersons' inquiries about my area of expertise, they would say: "I know some Arab American families who have children with disabilities" or "I am aware that a few Arab American children receive special education in a neighboring school." While writing this book, I was sitting at Panera Bread one evening with a friend whom I have known for the last 3 years. He is an Arab American who has lived in the United States for about 20 years. When he discovered that I was writing a book about Arab Americans with disabilities, he offered his help in arranging meetings for me with some Arab Americans who had family members with disabilities. He explained that he knew of several and that he would be happy to assist if I wanted to meet them.

As our conversation deepened, he told me that his cousin's son had autism. Then he explained to me that this child's parents or siblings have no problems whatsoever. He told me that his sister, who is in the early 40s, has a disability. From his description of her condition and the services she was receiving, I guessed that she had severe intellectual disability. He emphasized that his sister's condition was either the result of an X-ray to which she was exposed when their mother was pregnant with her or the result of a fall on her head that occurred when she was a baby. Here also, he asserted that his parents are not relatives, and nothing is wrong in the family. He told me that the only reason his aging parents never thought of going back to their native country was their daughter. He said, "Here [in the United States] she is being provided services and support that they can never dream of in their native country." I have met my friend's father several times. He is a very nice man in his early 80s, who I think receives Social Security disability benefits. My friend is a highly educated man in his mid 50s. His way of approaching disability, I believe, reflects fear of the strong social stigma attached to disability in Arab culture.

The purpose of this book is to provide special education and related service providers with basic information on Arab American children with disabilities, a population that has been largely neglected in literature pertaining to racial and ethnic minorities in special education in the United States. It offers an overview of Arab people, cultural values, disability issues, and culturally appropriate services for Arab American children with disabilities and their families. The book is divided into five chapters. Chapter 1 provides basic information about Arab Americans, including immigration; population size; educational, economic, and health status; religion; language; acculturation; stereotypes; and cultural traditions and practices. Because of lack of data on numbers and characteristics, Chapter 2 provides educated guesstimates about the prevalence rates of disabilities among Arab Americans. It also introduces basic information about Arab American families of children with disabilities, prominent Arab Americans with disabilities, and disability within the Arab culture.

In an effort to make navigating the special education system in the United States easier for Arab Americans, Chapter 3 provides a brief description of special education services as well as potential barriers to the use of these services by this population. Chapter 4 presents guidelines for providing culturally appropriate special education and related services for Arab American children with disabilities. Finally, Chapter 5 emphasizes the need and provides some directions for overcoming the gap in published literature pertaining to Arab Americans having disabilities.

1 Arab Americans

The purpose of this chapter is to offer a brief description of the Arab American population, which has become one of the fastest-growing ethnic populations in the United States. It emphasizes that though this population shares numerous commonalities, it is an enormously heterogeneous ethnic group. Then the chapter proceeds with a brief description of Arab American immigration to the United States. The chapter also describes the educational, economic, and health characteristics of Arab Americans; addresses issues related to this population's religious affiliation, language, and acculturation into the American culture; and discusses negative stereotypes of Arabs and the Arab American family system and cultural traditions. In the last section, an overview of disability in Arab countries is provided.

Who Are Arab Americans?

Arab Americans trace their ancestral roots to several Arab countries. The website of the American-Arab Anti-Discrimination Committee (ADC) describes Arabs as follows:

> Arabs are united by culture and by history. Arabs are not a race. Some have blue eyes and red hair; others are dark skinned; many are somewhere in between. Most Arabs are Muslims, but there are also millions of Christian Arabs and thousands of Jewish Arabs.

The Arab world should not be confused with the term *Middle East*, which denotes Arab and non-Arab countries, such as Israel, Iran, and Turkey. The Arab region stretches from the Atlantic Ocean in the west to the Arabian Sea in the east and from the Mediterranean Sea in the west to the Horn of Africa and the Indian Ocean in the southeast; it spans more than 13 million square kilometers (5 million square miles). The 22 Arab countries are Algeria, Bahrain, Comoros, Djibouti, Egypt, Iraq, Jordan, Kuwait, Lebanon,

Libya, Mauritania, Morocco, Oman, Palestine, Qatar, Saudi Arabia, Somalia, Sudan, Syria, Tunisia, United Arab Emirates (UAE), and Yemen.

The total population of these countries in 2010 was 369.8 million (World Bank, 2014), or about 5% of the world's population. The population of the Arab region is still young, with 60% of the population under the age of 25 (United Nations Population Fund, 2013). Although people in Arab countries share common culture, history, language, and religion (Islam, which is the main religion in most countries), these countries are religiously, ethnically, and economically diverse.

Some Arab countries are monarchies; the others are republics. Although some Arab countries, especially Gulf Arab States (Saudi Arabia, Qatar, Bahrain, Sultanate of Oman, Kuwait, and United Arab Emirates) and Iraq, have substantial reserves of petroleum, other Arab countries have limited natural resources, and their economies are mostly developing.

The conflicts, social unrest, ethnic conflict, and political tensions in the Arab region have seriously hampered development efforts during the last six decades. Some of these conflicts have been resolved, but others remain ongoing. Published recently by the United Nations Development Program (2014), the Arab human development report has demonstrated that human development measures in Arab countries have lagged behind the global average. Arab countries were reported to be low in human development measures, such as life expectancy, health care, education quality, income, gender equality, and overall life satisfaction. According to this report, the Arab region lags behind the rest of world, not because of a lack of resources but because of a shortage of freedom, knowledge, and womanpower. This report indicated that human development measures in Arab countries have improved recently in terms of life expectancy and school enrollment, but with wide variations among countries. Authors of this report also asserted that conflict, youth unemployment, and inequality can potentially hamper human development in the Arab region now and in the future.

Low standards of living, high and rising unemployment rates, and a growing sense of exclusion, according to Hassine (2014), were among the many reasons that prompted the so-called Arab Spring of December, 2010. Millions of Arab people in Tunisia, Egypt, Yemen, Libya, Syria, Bahrain, and other countries rose to demand respect, dignity, freedom, and employment. This Arab Spring, however, turned to Arab Winter, as civil, nonviolent demonstrations were met with violent responses from authorities and counter-demonstrators leading to wars in some countries, such as Libya and Syria. The Syrian civil war, which began in 2011, has produced severe humanitarian disasters. Millions of Syrians have been either displaced or became refugees or were left in poor living conditions. According to the UNDP, the deprivations caused by war in Syria and conflict in some other Arab countries may cause lasting health problems and contribute to lost livelihood, undermining long-term capabilities (United Nations Development Program, 2014). Hassine (2014) stated that political unrest sweeping Arab countries has led to further economic and social deterioration.

Arab Americans are unrecognized as a federal minority group, making it impossible to determine the exact number of Americans with Arab roots. Although their exact numbers are unknown, most sources agree that the number of Americans of Arab descent has increased steadily over the past three decades (Brown, Guskin, & Mitchell, 2012; de la Cruz & Brittingham, 2003). Arab Americans constitute an ethnic group of Americans made up of several waves of immigrants from the 22 Arab countries in North Africa and Southwest Asia, which shared numerous commonalities (e.g., language, religion, history, and cultural and political tradition). Despite commonalities, the Arab American population is enormously diverse, having varying religious, educational, and socioeconomic backgrounds, and complex historical, cultural, and political identities (Arab American Institute, 2012; Arab American National Museum, 2012; Asi & Beaulieu, 2013; Brown et al., 2012; Goforth, 2011). According to Donovan (2013),

> Altogether, Arab Americans are heterogeneous with regard to religion, acculturation level, Arabic dialect, social class, education level, national origin, generation in the US, and immigration history. . . . Even within the same family, parents can come from different countries of origin and have different immigration, discrimination, and trauma experiences. . . . This variability in background among Arab Americans reflects their long and rich immigration history into the US. This immigration history has directly influenced their racial classification.
>
> (p. 9)

Like other ethnic and linguistic minorities, Arab Americans have enriched the diversity of American society; however, this population faces more difficulties than other minorities as a result of sweeping stereotypes and misconceptions. Arab Americans are exposed to similar negative stereotypes and discrimination and, as a less invisible group than other minorities, they are made more visible in a negative way by the anti-Arab perception in the media (Campbell-Wilson, 2012).

The vast majority of Arab Americans (82%) are U.S. citizens, with nearly two thirds born in the United States (Arab American Institute, 2014). Like other ethnic groups in the United States, Arab Americans seek to fulfill the American dream and want to assimilate into American society, while preserving the important parts of their native culture and traditions (Dwairy, 2006).

Arab Immigration to the United States

According to several scholars and organizations (e.g., Arab American Institute, 2012; Arab American National Museum, 2013; Foad, 2013; Kayyali, 2006), immigrants from Arab countries arrived in the United States in three major waves. This immigration most often occurred as a result of economic hardship, war, insecurity, or discrimination in their respective home countries.

First Wave (1880–1920)

The first wave, between the late 1800s and World War I, consisted mainly of immigrants from Syria, Lebanon, Palestine, and Jordan (then known as Greater Syria). Most immigrants in this wave were Christians who settled primarily in the Northeast and Midwest. They left their native countries in search of better economic opportunities. Most of them were unskilled single men who had left their families behind (Abraham, 1995). Shared religion with the host culture made it easy for them to assimilate into the American society (Ferguson, 2004).

Second Wave (1948–1965)

Very few Arabs immigrated during the interwar period marked by the economic depression and anti-immigrant sentiment. Immigration resumed, however, after the conclusion of World War II, but in smaller numbers than in the first wave. The 1948 Arab–Israeli War led many Palestinians to immigrate. This wave included large numbers of immigrants from Egypt. Unlike the early immigrants, this second wave included many more Muslims. This period also witnessed the arrival of many Arab professionals and university students (Abraham, 1995). Assimilation for this group was more difficult because of a lack of shared religious perspectives and worldviews (Abudabbeh, 2005; Ferguson, 2004).

Third Wave (1965–Present)

In the mid-1960s, a third wave of Arab immigration commenced; it continues to the present. This wave has included many professionals, entrepreneurs, and unskilled and semiskilled laborers. These immigrants are often fleeing political instability and wars engulfing their home countries (Abraham, 1995).

Population

Despite the debate over the exact number of Arab Americans, they have become one of the fastest-growing ethnic populations in the United States. According to the U.S. Census Bureau (2010), nearly 1.8 million Arab

Americans lived in the United States in 2010. Arab American organizations and scholars as well as others have asserted that this figure significantly undercounts the population. The Arab American Institute (2012) suggested that the number of Arab Americans is closer to 3.7 million. Reasons for the undercount may include the placement of and limits of the ancestry question, unevenly distributed ethnic groups, high levels of out-marriage among the third and fourth generations, and distrust or misunderstanding of government surveys among recent immigrants. Ahmad (2004) cited a general fear of authority or concern about possible stereotyping and bias as a factor in the reluctance of some Arab Americans to identify their Arab descent. In addition, the Census definition of "Arab ancestry" excludes some Arab League countries, such as Somalia and Sudan, as countries of origin (Wang, 2013).

Although Arab Americans are not counted separately in the race question on the U.S. Census, data on specific population characteristics are collected through the American Community Survey (ACS), an ongoing Census Bureau survey that samples a small percentage of the population every year. These characteristics have been described in some Census special reports, such as *The Arab Population: 2000* (de la Cruz & Brittingham, 2003); "*We the people of Arab ancestry in the United States*" (Brittingham & de la Cruz, 2005); and "*Arab Households in the United States: 2006–2010*" (Asi & Beaulieu, 2013).

Arab Americans live in all 50 states; however, two thirds are geographically concentrated in 10 states: California, Michigan, New York, Florida, Texas, New Jersey, Illinois, Ohio, Massachusetts, and Pennsylvania. About 94% live in metropolitan areas, and Los Angeles, Detroit, New York–New Jersey, Chicago, and Washington, DC, are the top six metro areas of Arab American concentration (Arab American Institute, 2012). Other characteristics of the Arab American population include the following (*100 Questions*, 2001; Arab American Institute, 2012; Asi & Beaulieu, 2013; de la Cruz & Brittingham, 2003):

- Fifty-four percent of Arab Americans are men.
- The Arab American population as a whole is quite young, with about one of four Arab Americans in the United States under the age of 18.
- Most Arab Americans are of Lebanese or Syrian origin, but the population of Egyptian, Palestinian, and Iraqi Americans has been growing steadily.
- The overwhelming majority of Arab Americans (94%) live in metropolitan areas.
- Economic differences exist within the Arab American community.
- The cities with largest Arab American populations are Los Angeles, Detroit, New York, Chicago, and Washington, DC.

- Arab American families are, on average, larger than non-Arab American families and smaller than families in Arab countries.
- Arab Americans typically marry at a younger age than non-Arabs.

Educational Attainment and School Experiences

Education is highly valued by Arabs and Arab Americans. Arab American families tend to have a focused priority on education and support their children, especially boys, in acquiring it. Early Arab immigrants (1880–1924) had very little formal education; however, they provided their children with educational opportunities in hopes of a better future (Arab American National Museum, 2012). After the early 1950s, many Arab immigrants arrived with a college education, and some came as students to obtain college degrees and then remained in the United States. Second-wave Arab immigrants included large numbers of students seeking higher education in the United States. Foreign-born Arab professionals overwhelmingly prefer the fields of engineering, medicine, pharmacy, and the sciences in general (El-Badry, 1994).

According to the U.S. Census Bureau (2010), Arab Americans, both native-born and immigrants, have a higher level of educational achievement than the average U.S. population. Eighty-seven percent of Arab Americans have at least a high school diploma, and more than 40% have a bachelor's degree or higher, compared to 28% of Americans at large. The Census also showed that 17% of Arab Americans have a postgraduate degree, compared to the national average of 10%. Of the population currently enrolled in school, 12% are in preschool and kindergarten, 56% are in elementary or high school, and 32% are enrolled in college or undertaking graduate studies (Arab American Institute, 2012).

Arab Americans students in U.S. schools, however, face the same challenges other immigrant groups face; but they may also face additional challenges as a result of negative stereotypes and misconceptions about their culture and religion if they are Muslims (Schwartz, 1999). Furthermore, the educational systems in Arab countries are unlike those in the United States, and that may pose unique challenges for new immigrants. Despite substantial variations among Arab countries, almost all education systems in the Arab region suffer from serious shortcomings. Faour and Muasher (2011) noted that Arab education systems do not prepare students to compete in today's global, democratic society. Al-Krenawi and Graham (2000) stated that many Arab schools use curricula that are based largely on rote learning and on remembering facts, thus discouraging individual creativity and independent critical thinking. Al-Krenawi and Graham (2000) added that educational systems in Arab countries encourage conformity and obedience to teachers, who are viewed as strong authority figures.

Wingfield and Karaman (1995) maintained that demeaning stereotypes of Arabs, especially among school teachers, can have negative effects on Arab American students' achievement, self-image, and mental health. They asserted that many American educators do not even perceive anti-Arab racism as a problem. Despite the multicultural philosophy that has prevailed in American education over the past decades, Wingfield and Karaman (1995) reported that many teachers and the public at large are not yet sufficiently sensitized to the problem of anti-Arab and anti-Muslim stereotyping. Although the heritage of many racial and ethnic minorities (e.g., African Americans, Hispanics, Native Americans, and Asia/Pacific Americans) is addressed in multicultural articles, books, and curriculum, Arabs and the Middle East are ignored (Wingfield & Karaman, 1995).

Aburumuh, Smith, and Ratcliffe (2009) found public school teachers lacking basic knowledge about the Arab and Muslim cultures. They stated that this limited knowledge "leads to erroneous assumptions, pernicious beliefs, negative stereotypes and, ultimately, barriers to students' education" (p. 21). In her article, Schwartz (1999) offered the following suggestions for providing supportive school environments for Arab American students in public schools:

- Acknowledge Arab culture and history and dispel myths and negative stereotypes about Arab.
- Make schools and classrooms welcoming places where Arab American students feel included.
- Represent the Middle East and Arabs accurately and fairly in the curriculum and school activities.
- Ensure that Arab American students are treated equitably and without prejudice by teachers and peers, and respond to incidents of racism and possible harassment of Arab American students.
- Respect the customs of the native culture and religion of Arab students.
- Include Arab culture in multicultural courses and activities, arrange for field trips to Arab community institutions, and include Arab contributions in film series.
- Invite Arab American families to familiarize students with the various groups' celebrations, food, and history.
- Provide professional development training and make available to school staff accurate resource materials about the Middle East, Islam, and Arab Americans.
- Familiarize students with Middle East culture, including Arab music, Arab art, photographs of Arab countries, and notable Arab Americans.
- Include Islam in school and class activities involving religious tolerance.
- Evaluate books used and discard those with misinformation about Arabs.

Work and Income

Similar to the national average, about 65% of Arab American adults were in the labor force in 2010. Nearly two-thirds of working Arab Americans were employed in managerial, professional, technical, sales, or administrative fields. Most Arab Americans worked in the private sector (88%), and 12% were government employees. Median income for Arab American households was $56,433 compared with $51,914 for all households in the United States. In 2010 also, about 11% of Arab Americans lived in poverty, a number slightly higher than the overall population (Arab American Institute, 2012; Wang, 2013).

Health Status

Relatively limited information is available about the health status of Arab Americans living in the United States. Several articles have been written about culturally appropriate health care for Arab Americans (e.g., Aboul-Enin & Aboul-Enin, 2010; Erickson & Al-Timimi, 2001; Hammad, Kysia, Raba, Hassoun, & Connelly, 1999; Hammoud, White, & Fetters, 2005), but empirically acquired information is scarce despite increased attention to the health of Arab Americans over the past two decades, resulting in the publication of some studies. Although the researchers generally used no representative samples of the Arab American population and provided mixed results, they provided enlightening information. For example, Arab Americans seem to be at high risk for hypertension, cardiovascular disease, overweight, tobacco use, cancer, and diabetes (El-Sayed & Galea, 2009; Jaber et al., 2003).

Research has also indicated that immigration and discrimination may be risk factors for several diseases among Arab Americans (El-Sayed & Galea, 2009; Jaber et al., 2003). In a study of the health status of Arab, Muslim, and Chaldean American communities in Michigan, Aswad and Hammad (2001) found that 48% of respondents believed their health was equivalent to other communities, but 29% thought their community was healthier, and 23% perceived their health to be poorer. Nearly 80% of the respondents reported some form of insurance coverage, and 64% were unaware of free and available health services for women and children at local health departments or community centers. About 61% of the respondents stated that they exercised daily, 19% were on a diet to control an illness, 15% were smokers, and 7% drank alcohol.

Some researchers also investigated mortality, birth outcomes, and drug abuse among Arab Americans. A study by El-Sayed, Tracy, Scarborough, and Galea (2011) indicated that Arab Americans are disadvantaged in health relative to Whites. Particularly, important disparities in mortality resulting from chronic and infectious diseases were found among Arab Americans compared to non-Arab and non-Hispanic Whites. These researchers encouraged public health departments in areas with significant numbers of Arab American to consider interventions aimed at addressing risk factors for chronic illnesses and curbing the spread of infectious diseases among members of this community. They also suggested that clinicians counsel their adult Arab American patients about modifiable risk factors for diabetes and cardiovascular disease.

Two studies assessing the prevalence and the determinants of adverse birth outcomes in Michigan showed women of Arab ancestry to be at lower risk for adverse birth outcomes (preterm birth and low birth weight) than the general U.S. population (El-Sayed & Galea, 2009). In a study of nationally representative data, Read, Amick, and Donato (2005) found no significant difference in self-rated health between Arab immigrants and U.S.-born Whites. This study also showed that Arab immigrants were less likely to report limitations in activity. In another study, Arfken, Kubiak, and Loch (2007) reported that Arab Americans were similar to other ethnicities in drug abuse in that abusers were predominately male, unemployed, and involved with the criminal justice system.

In an effort to better meet the health needs of Arab Americans, several community organizations implemented programs aimed at improving care providers' understanding of the unique needs of Arab Americans and increasing this population's access to appropriate health services (e.g., Arab American Family Support Center, Arab Community Center for Economic and Social Services, Arab American Family Services, and National Arab American Medical Association).

Religious Affiliation

Although the majority of Arab Americans in the United States at the time of this writing descended from the first wave of mostly Christian immigrants, Arab Muslims represent the fastest-growing segment of the Arab American community (Arab American Institute, 2012). No religious information was asked in the 2000 U.S. census. According to the Arab American Institute (2012), the majority of Arab Americans are Christian. Specifically, 35% are Roman or Eastern Catholic, followed by Muslim (24%), Eastern Orthodox (18%), Protestant (10%), or other religions or no affiliations (13%).

Language

The Arabic language is the most single unifying feature among Arabs. Classical Arabic, also called Literary Arabic or Modern Standard Arabic, is used in writing and in most formal speech throughout the Arab World. Although most people understand it, Modern Standard Arabic is not used in conversations. Each national group (e.g., Lebanese, Palestinian, Syrian, Egyptian, Yemeni) has its particular dialect, and within each group are subdialects (Abraham, 1995). Local dialects, which vary among countries and regions, are not easily understood by those who speak another dialect; in addition, Arabic is not the only language spoken in the Arab world. Other non-Arabic languages are spoken in some parts of the Arab world; for example, Berber is commonly spoken in North Africa, and Kurdish is spoken in regions of Syria and Iraq. Assyrians and Chaldeans use a dialect of the original Aramaic language. Some Arab American families have been in the United States for generations and do not know Arabic (*100 Questions*, 2001). Many Arab people speak one or more languages other than Arabic; as a result of the colonization of Arab countries by the French and British, English and French are the two most commonly spoken foreign languages in Arab countries. Currently, school students in Arab countries are taught English or French as foreign languages. In 2000, the U.S. census showed that an estimated 50% of Arab Americans were bilingual, speaking a language other than English at home; however, 88% of those who spoke Arabic also spoke English well, demonstrating that most Arab Americans are willing and able to learn English without abandoning their native language (Samhan, n.d.). The census also ranked Arabic seventh among all foreign languages spoken by American school-aged children.

According to Martin (2009), Arab American children are often encouraged by their parents to learn Arabic, and in areas with high concentration of Arab Americans, some Muslim Arab American parents send their children to private schools that teach Arabic. The language gap may deter the involvement of recent Arab American immigrant parents in their children's schooling; furthermore, the traditional appearance of Muslim Arab American parents—if they maintain the use of distinctive dress in the United States—might be a particularly difficult feature for the school child to share with others (Hamdy, n.d.).

Arab communication styles tend to be formal, impersonal, and restrained (Al-Krenawi & Graham, 2000). Feghali (1997) reported that features of Arab communicative style include the following: (a) repetition (reiterations at the phonological, morphological and lexical, syntactic, and semantic levels); (b) elaboration (rich and expressive language use); and (c) affectiveness (affective style of emotional appeal). On the level of nonverbal and paralinguistic patterns, variations occur in gestural usage across Arab societies; however, Arabs generally tend to interact with a direct body orientation, stand close together, and touch frequently (within gender but not between genders).

An unidentified number of Arabic-speaking students are non-English proficient and learn English as a second language (ESL). The challenges faced by these students, which may be different from those faced by other minority ESL students resulting from linguistic and cultural differences (Akasha, 2013), have only recently received attention; furthermore, very little scientific research has been conducted by researchers to address these issues. The few research studies available on Arabic-speaking ESL students (Abdo & Breene, 2010; Akasha, 2013; Palmer, El-Ashry, Leclere, & Chang, 2007) revealed that among challenges faced by these students and their teachers are linguistic and cultural differences, lack of knowledge of Arab culture, negative stereotypes, lack of motivation, insufficient feedback and engagement, and lack of extra time for additional explanations.

Acculturation

Some studies have suggested that Arabs (especially those who are Muslim) find acculturation into the American culture to be more difficult than many other immigrant groups. Among factors that may have a negative impact on acculturation on all Arab American immigrants are (a) different cultural values, (b) exposure to negative stereotyped beliefs by the media, (c) relatively recent immigration history, and (d) tendency to be concentrated in specific regions of the United States (Abu-Qaoud, n.d.; Amer, 2005; Horan, 1996). For Muslims in particular, the main additional variable that may hinder acculturation to the dominant culture is their religious persuasion.

Acculturation has been shown to be an important factor in the well-being of Arab Americans, especially in their mental health (Jadalla & Lee, 2012). Amer (2005) found that assimilated Arab Americans experience less stress, anxiety, and depression compared to those who were separated or marginalized. In addition, Christian Arabs reported significantly less acculturative stress, anxiety, and depression compared to Muslim Arabs. Amer and Hovey (2007) found significant differences in patterns of acculturation between second-generation Muslim and Christian Arab Americans. Acculturation was found to be positively correlated with mental health among Christians, but not among Muslims. Horan (1996) reported that acculturation into American culture was much easier for Christian Arab Americans than for Muslim Arab Americans.

Goforth (2011) asserted that negative perceptions and acts of violence toward the Arab American community may pose an additional stress to its members; moreover, many Arab Americans, especially recent immigrants, experience acculturative stress during which mental health problems, such as anxiety and depression, frequently arise. According to Shalabi (2012), many

Arab Americans, whether native-born or newcomers, struggle to cope with two cultures. Many students maintain their heritage and at the same time fully interact with American society. Some may reject their culture, disassociate themselves from it, and try to fully adopt the host culture; other Arab Americans cling to their cultural heritage, rejecting assimilation into the dominant culture.

Stereotypes

Negative stereotypes of Arabs have historically been presented through the American media and popular culture in various forms (El-Farra, 1996; Erickson & Al-Timimi, 2001; Shaheen, 1984; Wingfield & Karaman, 1995). A recent poll conducted by the Arab American Institute (2014) revealed that Americans' opinions of Arabs have grown worse in recent years. This poll indicated that favorable attitudes toward Arabs dropped to 32% from 43% in 2010. The poll also showed that 42% of respondents believed law enforcement was justified in using profiling tactics against Arab Americans; furthermore, 57% of respondents reported feeling as if they knew little about Arab history or the people.

Many scholars (El-Farra, 1996; Shaheen, 2001) have reported widespread ignorance, bias, and misconceptions about Arabs, Arab Americans, and Muslims in popular culture and media. According to El-Farra (1996) and Shaheen (1984), the Western media have often presented Arabs in a negative and distorted manner (e.g., villains, culprits, terrorists, savages, untrustworthy, barbaric, fanatics, fabulously wealthy, and sex maniacs), creating a general mistrust and dislike of Arabs and a direct consequence upon Arab Americans nationwide. Nassar-McMillan (2011) stated that negative and inaccurate stereotypes of Arabs and Arab Americans are also found in educational texts and other media sources.

Table 1.1 provides additional helpful resources on Arab Americans for teachers and related services providers.

Erickson and Al-Timimi (2001) argued that denigration of Arab people is not discouraged in the United States, and stereotypes can have a negative impact on the development of a positive Arab American ethnic identity (see also Nassar-McMillan, 2011). Distorted perceptions and demeaning stereotypes are limiting and hurtful and can fuel fear and hatred of Arab and Muslim Americans; furthermore, such stereotypes degrade and dehumanize Arab identity and pride. Zoghby (as cited in Wisniewski, 2014) added that negative attitudes towards Arabs and Muslims affect their ability to function as communities. Numerous reports published over the last decade have revealed that hate crimes targeting Arab Americans and Muslims increased noticeably after the terrorist attacks of September 11, 2001, and the U.S.-led invasion of Iraq in 2003.

Although some truth may be associated with certain stereotypes of Arabs, many do not. Many improvements have been made with regard to the

Table 1.1 Resources

Helpful Online Resources

American-Arab Anti-Discrimination Committee (www.adc.org) is a civil rights organization committed to defending the rights of Arab Americans and promoting their cultural heritage.

Arab America Michigan (www.arabamerica.com/michigan) attempts to promote an accurate image about the Arab American community and the Arab world. Other primary goals of Arab America include bringing together the diverse Arab American community and serving as an educational resource site for all Americans.

Arab American Institute (www.aaiusa.org) strives to empower the Arab American community and promote its concerns. It also supports programs that promote awareness of Arab Americans and serves as a main resource on the Arab American experience for the media, academia, government agencies, and the private sector.

Arab American Center for Economic and Social Services (www.accesscommunity.org) strives to empower Arab American individuals, families, and communities to lead informed, productive, and culturally sensitive lives. ACCESS honors Arab American heritage through community building and service to all those in need.

Arab American Chamber of Commerce (www.arrabchamber.org) promotes and empowers the Arab American business community, supports its members, and provides them with valuable business solutions to ensure the growth and prosperity of their businesses.

Arab American National Museum (www.arabamericanmuseum.org) documents, preserves, and presents the history, culture, and contributions of the Arab American community. The Museum also strives to dispel stereotypes about Arab Americans.

National Arab American Medical Association (www.naama.com) offers continuing medical education credits to physicians, supports professional and educational activities aimed at health education and disease prevention, and sponsors national and international medical conventions or symposia.

Network of Arab-American Professionals (www.naaponline.org) promotes professional networking among Arab American professionals, raising awareness of Arab culture, identity, and concerns, serving Arab American communities through outreach programs.

elimination of racial and ethnic stereotypes from the American media, but stereotyping of Arabs has not declined: instead, it has actually increased in quantity and virulence (Shaheen, 2001). The most widely held myth of all is that Arab people (about 370 million) are all the same, but talking about them as one single monolithic group is completely incorrect. Myths and stereotypes about Arabs and Arab Americans that are repeated in American popular culture and the media are presented in Table 1.2.

Table 1.2 Myths and Facts About Arabs and Arab Americans

Myth	Fact
Most Arab people are nomads, live in tents, and ride camels.	This Arabic way of life was common hundreds of years ago, but it is rare today. Currently, nomadic people make up only about 2% of Arab people. Camel riding is rare and is used as tourist attraction or for sportive purposes.
Arab countries are nothing but desert and oil.	The geography of Arab countries is diverse. Some Arab countries are oil rich, but many have little or no oil reserves.
All Arabs are wealthy oil men.	Oil-producing countries (e.g., Saudi Arabia, Qatar, United Arab Emirates, Kuwait) are rich, but most Arab countries are not. In fact, very few Arabs have grown wealthy from oil, and the poverty rate is high in many Arab countries.
All people in Arab countries speak Arabic.	In addition to Arabic, Arab people speak many different languages and dialects in Arab countries, for example, Kurdish and Berber. English and French are widely spoken in some Arab countries.
Arab Americans are mainly Muslims.	Although a vast majority of the Arab world is Muslim, most Arab Americans are Christians; nonetheless, similar cultural traditions and practices are shared by Christian and Muslim Arabs.
All Arabs are Muslims.	Many Arabs are not Muslim. Several different Arab Christian groups can be found in various Arab countries (Lebanon, Egypt, Iraq, Syria, Jordan, Palestine).
Arab people are uneducated.	Arab people place a high value on education. Parents want their children, boys and girls alike, to have a good education. Although literacy rates vary from country to country, over 80% of the people in Arab countries are literate.
The Arab world is backward and uncivilized.	The Middle East is the cradle of civilization. The Arab region is a highly developed culture and civilization.
All Arab women are veiled.	According to teachings of Islam, women are supposed to wear veils; however, covering is not universally observed by Muslim women.
Arab women are subservient to men.	Arab women, like women all over the world, struggle against discrimination, inequality, and restrictions of their freedoms and rights based on cultural and religious beliefs; however, submissiveness is not an innate character trait of Arab women.

Sources: *Arab Cultural Awareness* (2006); *Common Misconceptions and Stereotypes* (2013); Goforth (2011).

Arab American Family and Culture

Given that Arab culture has enjoyed thousands of years of recorded history and that about 370 million Arabs currently inhabit 22 countries spread over expansive parts of North Africa and the Middle East, describing Arab culture in few pages is difficult; therefore, the intent here is to give very brief information about some of the various aspects of Arab culture. The information presented in this section should be used cautiously to avoid stereotyping Arab families or culture.

In *The Arab Family and the Challenge of Change*, Barakat (1993) stated that "the family is the basic unit of social organization in traditional and contemporary Arab society. At the center of social and economic activities, it is a relatively cohesive social institution" (p. 97). In this book published more than 20 years ago, Barakat emphasized that the Arab "family has been undergoing significant change and needs to be examined in the context of the transitional nature of Arab society" (p. 97). In fact, the family, which has historically been the most cherished aspect of Arab culture, has undergone an even more significant transformation in recent years. Family roles, size, relations, and decision making are all changing; nonetheless, gender and age are still the two most important factors that determine roles of family members in Arab culture.

The Arab family structure has changed in the last few decades as a result of industrialization, urbanization, war and unrest, and education, among other factors. Regardless, for the majority of Arabs "the family remains the main system of support throughout the Arab world and for Arabs living elsewhere" (Abudabbeh, 2005, p. 427). This is also true of Arab Americans. Abudabbeh (2005) noted, "The family is the cornerstone of the Arab American culture. There may be differences from one country to another in the intensity of the centrality of the family, but not in its impact on the dynamics of the family" (p. 430).

American families with Arab roots tend to maintain extended family networks. These families usually live near one another, spend considerable amounts of time together, and are intimately involved in one another's lives (Abraham, 1995). Nassar-McMillan (2011) noted, "Even fourth- or fifth-generation Arab Americans, although much more likely to be married to non-Arab Americans, often uphold the value of collectivism and community and utilize their large, extended families as support networks" (p. 37). Hence, unlike American and other Western societies, which are generally individualistic, Arab societies are overall collective, in which the family unit is of greater importance than the individual (Abadeh, 2006; Dwairy, 2006). Furthermore, Arab American culture is characterized by some basic values that differ from those held by most people in the United

States. These values involve premarital sex, cohabitation, child-rearing approaches, gender roles, religious preferences, nuclear or one-parent families, privacy, male–female relationships, family and social ties, and caring for elderly parents. In Table 1.3, the main attributes of the Arab culture are summarized.

Table 1.3 Main Characteristics of Arab Culture

1. The overwhelming majority of Arabs are Muslims; however, not all Arabs are Muslims, nor are all Muslims Arabs. More than 1.6 billion Muslims live all over the world, but less than 20% of them are Arabs.

2. The Arab region represents a rich culture and civilization; Arabs have made significant contributions in mathematics, astronomy, architecture, engineering, and music.

3. The various types of political systems in Arab countries include parliamentary republics and traditional monarchies or constitutional monarchies.

4. The family is the foundation of Arab society, and family honor is most important.

5. Arab societies are patriarchal and hierarchal: fathers and elders dominate.

6. In the Arab family, the father is the authority figure, and the mother has power over the house and the children.

7. Children belong to their father's family.

8. Children seldom live on their own until they marry.

9. In Arab societies, male offspring are favored.

10. More than 40% of the Arab population is under 15 years of age.

11. Religion for Arabs is central to everyday life.

12. Most Arabs believe that all life is controlled by the will of God (fate) instead of human beings.

13. Gender segregation is practiced to varying extents in various Arab countries.

14. Personal hygiene is extremely important to Arabs for both religious and practical reasons.

15. Arabs tend to use hand gestures when talking.

16. In several Arab countries, it is common for two men who are relatives, friends, or colleagues to hug and kiss both cheeks. Also common is cheek kissing between two women who know each other. Touching *between the opposite genders* in *public is considered obscene.*

17. Arabs consider advanced education a remarkable achievement and greatly respect scholars and educated men and women.

Sources: E. Donovan (2013); Farhat (2013); Feghali (1997); Nobles & Sciarra (2000); Obeidat, Shannak, Masa'deh, & Al-Jarrah (2012); Zaharna (1995).

For most Muslim Arab Americans, sex roles and intergender relations are important. Goforth (2011) noted:

> Traditionally, there are different expectations for females and males in Arab culture. . . . Girls and boys are expected to be physically separate and only have interactions if they are members of the same family. . . . Additionally, . . . being the opposite gender to the client may present some difficulties. . . . If possible, it may be more culturally appropriate to seek a colleague of the same gender to provide services.
>
> (p. 28)

Dating is rejected in Arab culture and occurs mainly among the most assimilated Arab Americans. Kayyali (2006) described dating among Arab Americans as follows:

> Although some girls accept their parents' concerns about dating, some bring the issue to the attention of their parents, negotiating a middle ground in which they are allowed to date if they introduce their dates to their parents first. Others rebel and date behind their parents' backs, and if their parents discover them, the situation could become violent, and stricter rules would likely be imposed.
>
> (pp. 73–74)

Most Arab American parents strongly encourage their children to marry someone from the same religious, ethnic, and socioeconomic background (Kayyali, 2012). Endogamous and arranged marriages, although decreased significantly in recent years, remain relatively common, especially among recent immigrant, less assimilated, and foreign-born Arab Americans (Abraham, 1995).

Arab culture is generally a high-contact culture in terms of physical contact and proximity. Arab people tend to stand closer to others during conversations than do Americans and other Westerners. A teacher who steps back to increase his or her personal space can unknowingly send an offending message to an Arab parent or student.

Persons of the same sex kiss each other on the cheek, hug, shake hands, hold hands, and stand close to one another. These are signs of affection without any sexual connotation. Zaharna (1995) described Arab communication patterns as high context (meaning is found more in the context than in the code, so messages are less specific and explicit), and indirect (ambiguous and emotional). Hammoud et al. (2005) cautioned service providers, asserting that some Muslims . . . may not shake hands with someone of the opposite sex. . . . In addition, patting [an individual's] arm or giving a woman a comforting hug should be avoided, unless the provider is of the same gender.

(p. 1308)

Arab clothing can be as varied as the persons wearing it and is influenced by several factors, such as ethnicity, education, socioeconomic status, geographic location, and the wearer's religious beliefs. Although the majority of Arabs are Muslims, a large number of Arab Christians live in Egypt, Lebanon, Syria, Palestine, Iraq, and Jordan. In general, Muslim clothing for both women and men is based on the principle of modesty. Nassar-McMillan (2011) clarified:

Modest dress, . . . prescribed for Muslim men and women, seeks to safeguard individuals from external influences, such as sexual harassment and other forms of disrespect. This norm, too, may be enforced more in traditional ethnic enclaves of Arab Americans than in countries of origin. It should be noted that Islamic dress for males includes loose fitting clothing, so as not to accentuate the body, and covering the body at least from navel to knee.

(pp. 39–40)

Muslim women's attire is not too form-fitting or sheer; no part of a woman's body should be seen except her face and hands. The hair is covered with a hijab or scarf. Some conservative Muslim women also cover their faces; however, many Arab women in countries such as Lebanon, Egypt, Jordan, Iraq, and Syria wear Western-style clothes, including jeans, shirts, and skirts. Men's clothing also depends on their native country and whether they live in a rural or urban area. Many Arab men wear Western-style clothes and some (especially citizens of Gulf Arab States) wear traditional ankle-length garment called *dishdasha* or *thawb*. Some Arab men also cover their heads with *kufiya* (also known as *ghutrah, shemagh,* or *hatta*), which is a traditional Middle Eastern headdress usually made of cotton. With the exception of some Muslim Arab American women who wear head scarves and long dresses and traditional clothing worn by both men and women on special occasions, Arab Americans generally do not wear traditional Arab clothing.

Food is an integral element of the cultural identity of Arabs as well as Arab Americans (Arab American National Museum, 2013). Essential to any cooking for Arabs is the concept of hospitality and generosity. Arab cuisine commonly focuses on meat (especially lamb and chicken), dairy products, herbs and spices—hot and to a lesser extent—as well as beverages, grains, fruits and vegetables, nuts, greens, olive oil, and sauces. Muslim Arabs eat only Halal meat (meat from animals slaughtered according to Islamic tradition). According to Islamic teachings, Muslims should not consume pork. Alcohol is also forbidden in Islam; however, some Arab Muslims drink alcohol openly or secretly.

Notably, most cultural guidelines for service providers focus on the Muslim identity of Arabs, thus overlooking Christians who represent the majority of Arab Americans (Khamis-Dakwar & Froud, 2012). Although all Arabs, both Muslims and Christians, are influenced by Islamic values and cultural traditions, especially those regarding gender roles and family relations (Read, 2003), psychological studies have revealed differences in acculturation and gender roles between Christian and Muslim Arab Americans (Ferguson, 2004; Khamis-Dakwar & Froud, 2012). Thus, additional research may be needed to identify the differences and similarities between these two religious groups.

References

100 questions and answers about Arab Americans. (2001). Retrieved from www. bintjbeil.com/E/ news/100q/home.html

Abadeh, H. (2006). *Perceptions of Arab American parents with children with special needs regarding home–school communications* (Doctoral dissertation). Retrieved from ProQuest Dissertations and Theses database. (UMI No. 304972765).

Abdo, I. B., & Breene, G. (2010). Teaching EFL to Jordanian students: New strategies for enhancing English acquisition in a distinct Middle Eastern student population. *Creative Education, 1*(1), 39–50.

Aboul-Enin, B. H., & Aboul-Enin, F. H. (2010). The cultural gap delivering health care services to Arab American populations in the United States. *Journal of Cultural Diversity, 17*(1), 20–23.

Abraham, N. (1995). Arab Americans. In R. J. Vecoli, J. Galens, A. Sheets, & R. V. Young (Eds.), *Gale encyclopedia of multicultural America* (Vol. 1, pp. 84–98). New York, NY: Gale Research.

Abudabbeh, N. (2005). Arab families: An overview. In M. McGoldrick, J. Giordano, & N. Garcia-Preto (Eds.), *Ethnicity and family therapy* (3rd ed., pp. 423–436). New York, NY: Guilford Press.

Abu-Qaoud, M. (n.d.). *The acculturation of Arab immigrants in the US.* Retrieved from ethics.sandiego.edu/Courses/HNRS150/M.Abu-Qaoud.ppt

Aburumuh, H. A., Smith, H. L., & Ratcliffe, L. G. (2009). *Educators' cultural awareness and perceptions of Arab-American students: Breaking the cycle of ignorance.* Retrieved from libra.msra.cn/. . ./running-head-educators-awareness-and-perceptions-of-ara

Ahmad, N. (2004). *Arab-American culture and health care.* Retrieved from www. cwru.edu/med/epidbio/mphp439/Arab-Americans.htm

Akasha, O. (2013). Exploring the challenges facing Arabic-speaking ESL students and teachers in middle school. *Journal of ELT and Applied Linguistics, 1*(1), 12–31.

Al-Krenawi, A., & Graham, J. R. (2000). Culturally sensitive social work practice with Arab clients in mental health settings. *Health & Social Work, 25*(1), 9–22.

Amer, M. M. (2005). *Arab American mental health in the post September 11 era: Acculturation, stress, and coping* (Doctoral dissertation). Retrieved from http://utdr.utoledo.edu/cgi/viewcontent.cgi?article=2424&context=theses-dissertations

Amer, M. M., & Hovey, J. D. (2012). Anxiety and depression in a post-September 11 sample of Arabs in the USA. *Social Psychiatry and Psychiatric Epidemiology, 47*(3), 409–418.

Arab American Institute. (2012). *Demographics.* Retrieved from www.aaiusa.org/pages/demographics

Arab American Institute. (2014). *Poll shows Americans' views of Arabs, Muslims have gotten worse.* Retrieved from www.aaiusa.org/index_ee.php/news/entry/poll-shows

Arab American National Museum. (2012). *Arab Americans: An integral part of American society.* Retrieved from www.arabamericanmuseum.org/umages/pdfs/resource_booklets/AANM-ArabAmericansBooklet-web.pdf

Arab American National Museum. (2013). *Arab American culture.* Retrieved from www.arabamericanmuseum.org/Arab+American+Culture.id.168.htm

Arab cultural awareness: 58 factsheets. (2006). Retrieved from fas.org/irp/agency/army/arabculture.pdf

Arfken, C. L., Kubiak, S. P., & Farrag, M. (2009). Acculturation and polysubstance abuse in Arab-American treatment clients. *Transcultural Psychiatry, 46*(4), 608–622.

Asi, M., & Beaulieu, D. (2013). Arab households in the United States: 2006–2010. *American Community Survey Briefs, U.S. Census Bureau.* Retrieved from www.census.gov/prod/2013pubs/acsbr10–20.pdf

Aswad, M., & Hammad, A. (2001). *Health survey of the Arab, Muslim, and Chaldean American communities in Michigan.* Retrieved from www.accesscommunity.org/sites/default/files/documents/health_and_research_cente_19.pdf

Barakat, H. (1993). *The Arab family and the challenge of change.* Oakland, CA: University of California Press.

Brittingham, A., & de la Cruz, C. P. (2005). We the people of Arab ancestry in the United States. *Census 2000 Special Reports.* Retrieved from www.census.gov/prod/2005pubs/censr-21.pdf

Brown, H., Guskin, E., & Mitchell, A. (2012). *Arab-American population growth.* Retrieved from www.journalism.org/2012/11/28/arabamerican-population-growth/

Campbell-Wilson, F. (2012). Middle East and Arab American cultures. In D. E. Battle (Ed.), *Communication disorders in multicultural and international populations* (4th ed., pp. 61–75). St. Louis, MO: Mosby.

Common misconceptions and stereotypes about the Middle East. (2013, October 21). Seattle, WA: Henry M. Jackson School of International Studies, University of Washington. Retrieved from http://jsis.washington.edu/outreach/file/Country%202pagers/THEME%20PAGES/Mideast%20misconceptions.pdf

de la Cruz, G. P., & Brittingham, A. (2003). *The Arab population: 2000.* Washington, DC: U.S. Census Bureau. Retrieved from www.census.gov/prod/2003pubs/c2kbr-23.pdf

Donovan, E. (2013). *A phenomenological exploration of Arab American parents' experiences with the special education process* (Doctoral dissertation). Retrieved from https://etd.ohiolink.edu/ap:0:0:APPLICATION_PROCESS=DOWNLOAD_ETD_SUB_DOC_ACCNUM:::F1501_ID:kent1372583897,inline

Dwairy, M. (2006). *Counseling and psychotherapy with Arabs and Muslims: A culturally sensitive approach.* New York, NY: Teachers College Press.

El-Badry, S. (1994). The Arab-Americans. *American Demographics, 75*(1), 22–30.

El-Farra, N. (1996). Arabs and the media. *Journal of Media Psychology, 1*(2), 1–9.

El-Sayed, A. M., & Galea, S. (2009). The health of Arab-Americans living in the United States: A systematic review of the literature. *BMC Public Health, 9,* 272–280.

El-Sayed, A. M., Tracy, M., Scarborough, P., & Galea, S. (2011). Ethnic inequalities in mortality: The case of Arab Americans. *PLOS One, 6*(12). Retrieved from www.ncbi.nlm.nih.gov

Erickson, C. D., & Al-Timimi, N. R. (2001). Providing mental health services to Arab Americans: Recommendations and considerations. *Cultural Diversity and Ethnic Minority Psychology, 7*(4), 308–327.

Faour, M., & Muasher, M. (2011). Education for citizenship in the Arab world: Key to the future. *Carnegie Middle East Center.* Retrieved from carnegieendowment.org/files/citizenship_education.pdf

Farhat, E. O. (2013). Gender, power, politeness and women in the Arab society. *International Journal of English Language & Translation Studies, 1*(1), 50–60.

Feghali, E. (1997). Arab cultural communication patterns. *International Journal of Intercultural Relations, 21*(3), 345–378.

Ferguson, C. J. (2004). Arab Americans: Acculturation and prejudice in an era of international conflicts. In C. Negy (Ed.), *Cross-cultural psychotherapy: Toward a critical understanding of diverse clients* (pp. 265–278). Reno, NV: Bent Tree Press.

Foad, H. S. (2013). *Waves of immigration from the Middle East to the United States.* Retrieved from papers.ssrn.com/sol3/papers.cfm?abstract_id=2383505

Goforth, A. N. (2011). Considerations for school psychologists working with Arab American children and families. *NASP Communique, 39*(6). Retrieved from www.nasponline.org/publications/cq/39/6/Multicultural-Affairs.aspx

Hamdy, K. (n.d.). *Arab and Muslim Americans: An introduction for educators.* Retrieved from www.cengage.com/resource_uploads/downloads/0495915297_257292.pdf

Hammad, A., Kysia, R., Rabah, R., Hassoun, R., & Connelly, M. (1999). *ACCESS guide to Arab culture: Health care delivery to the Arab American community.* Retrieved from www.naama.com/pdf/arab-american-culture-health-care.pdf

Hammoud, M. M., White, C. B., & Fetters, M. D. (2005). Opening cultural doors: Providing culturally sensitive healthcare to Arab American and American Muslim patients. *American Journal of Obstetrics and Gynecology, 193,* 1307–1311.

Hassine, N. B. (2014). *Economic inequality in the Arab region.* Retrieved from www-wds.worldbank.org/external/default/WDSContentServer/WDSP/IB/2014/06/09/000158349_20140609130102/Rendered/PDF/WPS6911.pdf

Horan, A. E. (1996). Arab-American communities and their acculturation into the American culture and society. *Dissertation Abstracts International, 57*(6-A).

Jaber, L. A., Brown, M. B., Hammad, A., Nowak, S. N., Zhu, Q., Ghafoor, A., & Herman, W. H. (2003). Epidemiology of diabetes among Arab Americans. *Diabetes Care, 26*(2), 308–313.

Jadalla, A., & Lee, J. (2012). The relationship between acculturation and general health of Arab Americans. *Journal of Transcultural Nursing, 23*(2), 159–165.

Kayyali, R. A. (2006). *The Arab Americans: A history*. Westport, CT: Greenwood Press.

Kayyali, R. A. (2012). The family. In A. Ameri & H. Arida (Eds.), *Daily life of Arab Americans in the 21st century* (pp. 57–86). Dearborn, MI: Arab American National Museum.

Khamis-Dakwar, R., & Froud, K. (2012). Aphasia, language, and culture: Arabs in the U.S. In M. R. Gitterman, M. Goral, & L. K. Obler (Eds.), *Aspects of multilingual aphasia* (pp. 275–291). Hayward, CA: Bristol.

Martin, N. (2009). *Arab American parents' attitudes toward their children's heritage language maintenance and language practices* (Master's thesis). Retrieved from ProQuest Dissertations and Theses database. (UMI No. 1472860).

Nassar-McMillan, S. (2011). *Counseling and diversity: Counseling Arab Americans*. Belmont, CA: Brooks/Cole.

Nobles, A. Y., & Sciarra, D. T. (2000). Cultural determinants in the treatment of Arab Americans: A primer for mainstream therapists. *American Journal of Orthopsychiatry, 70*(2), 182–191.

Obeidat, B., Shannak, R., Masa'deh, R., & Al-Jarrah, I. (2012). Toward better understanding for Arabian culture: Implications based on Hofstede's cultural model. *European Journal of Social Sciences, 28*(4), 512–522.

Palmer, B. C., El-Ashry, F., Leclere, J. T., & Chang, S. (2007). Learning from Abdallah: A case study of an Arabic-speaking child in a U.S. school. *The Reading Teacher, 61*(1), 8–17.

Read, J. G. (2003). The sources of gender role attitudes among Christian and Muslim Arab-American women. *Sociology of Religion, 64*(2), 207–222.

Read, J. G., Amick, B., & Donato, K. M. (2005). Arab immigrants: A new case for ethnicity and health? *Social Science and Medicine, 61*(1), 77–82.

Samhan, H. (n.d.). By the numbers. *Allied Media Corp*. Retrieved from www.alliedmedia.com/Arab-American/Arab_demographics.htm

Schwartz, W. (1999). Arab American students in public schools. *ERIC Digests* (ED 429144). Retrieved from http://iume.tc.columbia.edu/i/a/document/15693_Digest_142.pdf

Shaheen, J. G. (1984). *The TV Arab*. Bowling Green, OH: Bowling Green State University Popular Press.

Shaheen, J. G. (2001). *Reel bad Arabs: How Hollywood vilifies a people*. Brooklyn, NY: Olive Branch Press.

Shalabi, L. (2012). *The identity crisis of Arab American students in American public schools*. Retrieved from www.arabstereotypes.org/blog/201202/15–405

United Nations Development Program. (2014). *Arab human development report*. Retrieved from www.arab-hdr.org

United Nations Population Fund. (2013). *A platform for voices of Arab youth in a critical time*. Retrieved from www.unfpa.org/news/platform-voices-arab-youth-critical-time

U.S. Census Bureau. (2010). *American community survey 1-year estimates*. Retrieved from www.census.gov/acs/www

Wang, H. L. (2013). *Arab-Americans: A 'growing' community, but by how much?* Retrieved from www.npr.org/blogs/codeswitch/2013/05/30/187096445

Wingfield, M., & Karaman, B. (1995). Arab stereotypes and American educators. *Social Studies and the Young Learner, 7*(4), 7–10. Retrieved from www.adc.org/index.php?id=283

Wisniewski, M. (2014). *Poll: American opinion of Arabs, Muslims is getting worse.* Retrieved from http://english.alarabiya.net/en/perspective/analysis/2014/07/30/Poll-American-opinion-of-Arabs-Muslims-is-getting-worse.html

World Bank. (2014). *Arab world.* Retrieved from http://data.worldbank.org/region/ARB

Zaharna, R. S. (1995). Understanding cultural preferences of Arab communication patterns. *Public Relations Review, 21*(3), 241–255.

Further Readings

Al-Hazza, T., & Lucking, R. (2005). The minority of suspicion: Arab Americans. *Multicultural Review, 14*(3), 32–38.

Al-Mateen, C. S. (2004). The Muslim child, adolescent, and family. *Child and Adolescent Psychiatric Clinics of North America, 13*(1), 183–200.

Haddad, Y. Y. (2004). *Not quite American? The shaping of Arab and Muslim identity in the United States.* Waco, TX: Baylor University Press.

Hassoun, R. (2005). *Arab Americans in Michigan.* Ethnicity in Michigan series. East Lansing: Michigan State University Press.

Jamal, A. A. (2008). *Race and Arab Americans before and after 9/11: From invisible citizens to visible subjects.* Syracuse, NY: Syracuse University Press.

Kasem, C. (2001). *Arab-Americans: Making a difference.* Retrieved from www.freerepublic.com/focus/f-news/590960/posts

Naber, N. (2000). Ambiguous insiders: An investigation of Arab American invisibility. *Ethnic and Racial Studies, 23*(1), 37–61.

Sulaiman, M. (2008). Mental health issues of Arab American youth. Paper presented at the *American Experience: A National Summit to Promote the Well-being of Arab and Muslim Youth,* Dearborn, MI.

Suleiman, M. W. (1999). *Arabs in America: Building a new future.* Philadelphia, PA: Temple University Press.

Suleiman, M. W. (2000). *Teaching about Arab Americans: What social studies teachers should know.* (ERIC Document Reproduction Service No. ED442 714).

Weaver, K. (2010). *Arab Americans and segmented assimilation: Looking beyond the theory to the reality in the Detroit Metro Area.* Master's thesis. Retrieved from www.duo.uio.no/bitstream/handle/123456789/26217/thesis.pdf

Yahya, H. A. (2010). *Arab American students in USA schools.* Retrieved from www.articlesbase.com/ . . . /arab-american-students-in-usa

Zogby, J. (1998). The politics of exclusion. *Civil Rights Journal, 3*(1), 42–48.

2 Disability Among Arab Americans

This chapter begins with highlighting the little attention that this minority has received so far in the research literature pertinent to racial/ethnic minorities with disabilities in the United States. Then, it provides educated guesstimates about the prevalence rates of disabilities among Arab Americans. The chapter also presents information regarding Arab American families having members with disabilities and disability in Arab culture, and it introduces some distinguished Arab Americans with disabilities.

A Forgotten Subminority

Arab Americans with disabilities are a forgotten subminority of an ethnic minority that has been described as "marginalized and overwhelmed with untrue stereotypes" (Lake, 2014). Whether in literature pertinent to racial/ethnic minorities with disabilities or in literature related to Americans of Arab ancestry, Arab American persons with disabilities have generally been forgotten. Little attention has been given to disability among Arab Americans in the United States, and numbers of Arab Americans having disabilities remain unknown (Abadeh, 2006; Donovan, 2013). Commenting on disability among Arab Americans, Campbell-Wilson (2012) stated that although the prevalence of disability has been documented for various racial and ethnic groups, little attention has been paid to Arab Americans in the United States. The only study that involved disability prevalence in older Arab Americans was an analysis of data from a sample of the 2000 U.S. Census conducted by Dallo, Snih, and Ajrouch (2009). This study indicated that immigrant Arab Americans had a higher prevalence rate of both physical and self-care disabilities compared to U.S.-born Arab Americans. Immigrant status has also been shown to be significant concerning Arab American health. Using data from the 2003 Detroit Arab American Study, Abdulrahim and Baker (2009) examined the self-rated health of Arab Americans. The results revealed that Arab immigrants were more likely to report poorer self-related health compared to U.S.-born Arab Americans; however, Read, Amick, and Donato (2005) found no differences between U.S.-born and immigrant Arab Americans in self-rated health. Still, many studies concluded that immigrant status may be associated positively or negatively with Arab Americans' health status (El-Sayed & Galea, 2009). Studies also revealed that better health status of Arab Americans was associated with both acculturation and English language proficiency (Abdulrahim & Baker, 2009; El-Sayed & Galea, 2009). Hence, one cannot predict health status or disability prevalence in light of immigrant status.

How Many Arab Americans Have Disabilities?

Estimating the number of Arab Americans with disabilities is a daunting undertaking for at least three reasons: first, the U.S. Census does not use an Arab American classification. As mentioned in Chapter 1, Arab Americans are excluded from the U.S. Census Bureau reports pertaining to the Census of Population and Housing. Instead, people of Arab descent are classified under the "White" or "Some Other Race" category (Hixson, Hepler, & Kim, 2011) in surveys using federal standards for race and ethnicity; thus, knowing the numbers of Arab Americans is extremely difficult (Arab American Institute, 2012). Second, reports on the prevalence of disabilities, which focus on the major racial and ethnic groups, understandably, do not mention Arab Americans with disabilities. Third, disability prevalence is influenced by general health, the social environment, and other factors such as economic conditions, social mores, culture and available resources, demographic factors, and environmental factors (World Health Organization, 2011), and little information is available on these factors with regard to the Arab American population.

Given the growth of this population over the past two decades, it is expected that special educators and other service providers are increasingly likely to work with Arab American students with disabilities and their parents (Donovan, 2013; Goforth, 2011; Haboush, 2007). According to Abudabbeh (2005), an increasing number of Arab Americans have sought professional help and consultation recently for a variety of problems, including learning disabilities and attention-deficit/hyperactivity disorder, yet empirical knowledge on prevalence of disabilities among Arab Americans is lacking (Abadeh, 2006; Campbell-Wilson, 2012; Donovan, 2013). As noted previously, the only study that addressed this issue was conducted by Dallo et al. (2009), which used data from the 2000 U.S. Census to estimate the prevalence of physical disability and self-care disability among older Arab Americans (65 years of age and older).

Gharaibeh (2009) postulated that disability prevalence rates in Arab countries would be at least equivalent to that of the United States, if not higher. This author's judgment is based on features of Arab societies that contribute to high disability prevalence, such as consanguineous marriages, poverty, high illiteracy, poor health care, limited preventive programs, and armed conflicts; however, in light of the lack of data on the prevalence of disability among Arab Americans, the author attempted to develop a rough guesstimate of their numbers.

If the data on disability prevalence in the United States are applied to the Arab American population, an unadjusted rough estimate of the number of Arab Americans of all ages having disabilities ranges from 336,600 to 691,900, and the total number of Arab American school-aged children ranges from 23,400 to 48,200. The numbers of these persons in the top 10 states with the largest Arab American communities are shown in Table 2.1. These numbers are based upon the following data: (a) estimates of the number of Arab Americans range from 1.8 million (as reported by U.S. Census Bureau, 2010) to 3.7 million (as estimated by the Arab American Institute, 2012); (b) the prevalence rates of disability among the U.S. population represent 18.7% of the U.S. population of all ages and 5.2% of school-aged children (aged 5–17) as reported by Brault (2012); and (c) 25% of the Arab American population comprises school-aged children as reported by Frisby and Reynolds (2005) and Goforth (2011). Accordingly, the number of Arab American school-aged children ranges from 450,000, according to the U.S. Census Bureau (2010), and 925,000, according to Arab American Institute (2012) figures.

The estimates shown in Table 2.1 address disability as defined and classified by the American Community Survey carried out by the U.S. Census Bureau. In this Survey, *disability* was defined as follows:

> A person is considered to have a disability if he or she has difficulty performing certain functions (seeing, hearing, talking, walking, climbing stairs and lifting and carrying), or has difficulty performing activities of daily living, or has difficulty with certain social roles (doing school work for children, working at a job and around the house for adults). A person who is unable to perform one or more activities, or who uses an assistive device to get around, or who needs assistance from another person to perform basic activities is considered to have a severe disability.
>
> (U.S. Census Bureau, 1997)

Table 2.1 Rough Estimate of the Number of Arab Americans of All Ages and Arab
American School-Aged Children with Disabilities in the United States

State	Percentage of Total Arab American Population	Rough Estimate of the Number of Arab Americans with Disabilities per 2011 U.S. Census Population Figures		Rough Estimate of the Number of Arab Americans with Disabilities per 2012 Arab American Institute Population Figures	
		All Ages	School-Age	All Ages	School-Age
California	15	50,490	3,510	103,785	7,215
Michigan	11	37,026	2,574	76,109	5,393
New York	8	26,928	1,872	55,352	3,848
Florida	6	20,196	1,404	41,514	2,886
Texas	5	16,830	1,170	34,595	2,405
New Jersey	5	16,830	1,170	34,595	2,405
Illinois	5	16,830	1,170	34,595	2,405
Ohio	4	13,464	936	27,676	1,924
Massachusetts	4	13,464	936	27,676	1,924
Pennsylvania	3	10,098	702	20,757	1,443
Other States	34	114,444	7,956	235,246	16,354
All States	100	336,600	23,400	691,900	48,200

The American Community Survey includes six types of disability:

- Hearing difficulty: deaf or having serious difficulty hearing
- Vision difficulty: blind or having serious difficulty seeing, even when wearing glasses
- Cognitive difficulty: because of a physical, mental, or emotional problem, having difficulty remembering, concentrating, or making decisions
- Ambulatory difficulty: having serious difficulty walking or climbing stairs
- Self-care difficulty: having difficulty bathing or dressing
- Independent living difficulty: because of a physical, mental, or emotional problem, having difficulty doing errands alone such as visiting a doctor's office or shopping

Notably, the definitions and types of disability used in the U.S. Census differ from the definitions and types used by other sources (medical, social, or educational). Accordingly, estimates of the number of Arab Americans with disabilities depend on the definitions used in data collection. The

Individuals with Disabilities Education Act (IDEA), the U.S. federal law that governs the provision of special education and related services to children with disabilities, classifies disability into 14 categories: autism, deaf–blindness, deafness, developmental delay, emotional disturbance, hearing impairment, intellectual disability, multiple disabilities, orthopedic impairment, other health impairment, specific learning disability, speech or language impairment, traumatic brain injury, and visual impairment.

It is important to reemphasize here that the numbers presented in Table 2.1 are approximations made by the author because data necessary to make reliable disability prevalence rates among the Arab American population are lacking. These estimates were based on estimates of the numbers of Americans with Arab roots and disability prevalence rates in the United States. Obviously, scientific efforts to collect accurate information on the Arab American population size and disability prevalence among this population are needed.

Speech and Language Disorders

According to Campbell-Wilson (2012) speech, language, and hearing services for Arab Americans as well as for people with communication disorders in Arab countries have increased over the past two decades; however, a substantial dearth of services for Arab Americans having communication disorders remains. Reasons are varied and include but are not limited to lack of trained native Arab speech and language pathologists and audiologists, limited access to services, and limited educational support systems. Another important reason involves perception: although speech and language disorders can have deleterious psychological effects on a person in Arab society, the public does not perceive them as disabilities.

Learning Disabilities

The term *learning difficulties* emerged in educational circles in Arab countries in the 1980s. Until the 1950s and even during the 1960s, relatively few Arabs had the opportunity to enroll in schools. Because those having difficulty reading or writing or doing arithmetic had no schooling, their problems were never diagnosed. Unless they had significant psychosocial difficulties, they were not considered to have special or different needs. In Arab schools, some students have always had difficulties learning reading, writing, or mathematics; but remedial and special education services have been unavailable for an overwhelming majority of them until recently.

The Arab American Family Services in Bridgeview, Illinois, recently established a tutoring department to provide remedial education for Arab

American children struggling academically in school following an increase in the number of students in Grades 2 through 8 needing service. Coordinating with the local schools, the center provided individualized instruction in reading comprehension, spelling, writing, and math, but center personnel found that many of the children struggled in school because of a language barrier. Such children are often lost in the educational system and placed in special education programs. Many believe these children may have a learning disability, but in reality most of them merely lack English proficiency because their parents do not speak or understand the English language well.

Autism Spectrum Disorder

Olson (2013) reported University of Minnesota researchers' findings showing that autism spectrum disorder (ASD) rates among Minneapolis Somali community were higher than U.S. national averages (Somalia is a member of the League of Arab States). In addition, this study revealed that ASD was more severe in all Somali children enrolled in Minnesota schools. All of them had related intellectual disability. Further, Hijazi (2014) quoted an Arab American mother from Detroit who has two children with autism as saying:

> The Arab community needs to be more open with having a kid with any type of disability. They need to stop thinking that they will get better. Parents need to know what the signs are, and they need to know that it's okay. It's nothing to be ashamed of.

AlHajal (2009) reported about an Arab American car salesman whose son had ASD but who knew nothing about autism except for what he learned in the movie *Rain Man*. This father believed that lack of knowledge about autism in the Arab American community could prevent or delay diagnoses, leaving families confused and frustrated. AlHajal also interviewed the special events coordinator at a school for children with autism in Michigan who had been working with this group of children for over three decades; she reported that a growing number of Arab American families were turning to the school for help.

Physical Disabilities and Health Impairments

Dallo et al. (2009), as noted previously, found that foreign-born Arab Americans had a higher prevalence rate of physical disabilities (31.2%) and self-care disabilities compared to U.S.-born Arab Americans (23.4%). Arab immigrants also had higher self-care disabilities (13.5%) than U.S.-born Arab Americans

(6.8%). El-Sayed and Galea (2009) found little consensus in the medical literature about the prevalence and correlates of some chronic diseases, such as diabetes and cardiovascular diseases, among Arab Americans.

Health impairments are not counted in disability registries in Arab countries. Conditions like sickle cell anemia, cancer, HIV/AIDS, bronchial asthma, chronic obstructive pulmonary disease, and diabetes, among others, are regarded as chronic illnesses that are the sole responsibility of health care providers. Physical disabilities as defined in disability surveys in Arab countries are generally confined to paralysis (like in cerebral palsy, spina bifida, and spinal cord injuries) and amputations. Most other forms of neurological and musculoskeletal disorders are similarly not included in disability registries; nonetheless, physical disabilities and health are also less stigmatized than other types of disabilities (e.g., intellectual disabilities) in Arab countries. Students with physical disabilities and health impairments have always been included in regular schools and universities in the region, except when they have additional disabilities. For the most part, these students are not considered eligible for special education categories unless they have other disabling conditions.

Hearing Impairments

In their review of literature related to the health of Arab Americans in the United States, El-Sayed, Tracy, Scarborough, and Galea (2011) did not cite any study pertinent to ear problems or hearing impairments in this community. Interfamily marriage is still common among Arabs and can be found among Arab Americans; however, this practice has decline among highly assimilated and native-born Arab Americans as well as educated people (Abraham, 1995). Parental consanguinity has been shown to correlate with hearing loss in children (Bener, ElHakeem, & Abdulhadi, 2005). To the best of this author's knowledge, no research has been published about correlates of hearing impairment caused by otitis media (middle ear infection), aging, and loud noise with illnesses like meningitis among Arab Americans. Similarly, nothing has been published on educational achievement, interpretation services, psychosocial adjustment, or employment of Arab Americans who are deaf or hard of hearing.

Unless hearing loss is accompanied by muteness, a person with a hearing impairment in the Arab region is accepted by others with little difficulty. Although no shared common sign language is used in the region, sign languages unrelated historically with some similarities in their vocabularies can be found due the sharing of similar cultural values and gestural repertoires (Al-Fityani & Padden, 2010). In a recent development related to sign language use by Muslims, Global Deaf Muslim (GDM), set up by a young Muslim man from Ghana now living in Virginia, has worked to raise $480,000 to fund translation of the Qur'an (the holy book of Islam) into American Sign Language (Global Deaf Muslim, 2014). GDM also advocates for an accessible and inclusive Muslim community of all Muslims and the advancement of interpretation services at mosques (places of worship for Muslims).

Various national sign languages are used in Arab countries, none of which are well developed. An attempt is currently underway to adopt a unified Arab sign language; however, the system under development focuses on vocabulary but does not include grammar. Overall, deaf persons from Arabic-speaking countries learn American sign language well. Some schools for the deaf in the Arab region have introduced American sign language to its students; the Moroccan sign language was, in fact, derived from the American sign language.

Visual Impairments

The survey of health of Arab Americans in the United States conducted by El-Sayed et al. (2011) mentioned previously, also included no research on eye diseases or visual impairments among Arab Americans. Nonetheless, the disability type that is least stigmatized in the Arab region is blindness. Although giving a specific explanation is difficult, reasons may be embedded in the Arab history and Arabic and Islamic cultures. Historically, some blind Arab persons have excelled in literature (e.g., Taha Hussein, Abu Alaa' Al Maa'rri, Bashar Ibn Burd); music (e.g., Ammar Al Shuray, Sayyed Mekawi, Sheikh Imam, Ibtisam Lutfi); and religion (e.g., Abdul Azeez Ibn Baz, Fadel Hasan Abbas, Abdul Hameed Kishk, Omar Abdul Rahman). Followers of Islam know a touching story of a blind man with Prophet Muhammad. One day that man, named Abdullah Ibn Umm Maktoum, approached the Prophet and interrupted him to ask something while he was explaining Islam to a group of people. The Prophet felt annoyed, and he frowned at Abdullah. In the Qur'an, God admonished his prophet for not paying attention to the blind man. After that chapter (sura), the Prophet used to greet Abdullah saying: "Welcome to him on whose account my sustainer has rebuked me."

In Arab countries, only blindness and very severe cases of visual impairment are captured by registration data. The majority of persons with low vision are not formally identified in schools and do not receive special support services. In other words, they are not considered persons with disabilities, unless visual loss is severe and has visible symptoms. Those who are formally diagnosed by ophthalmologists as having severe vision loss get the same treatment in schools as persons with blindness, but many persons with blindness are offended to be labeled as persons with disabilities. Only in the past two or three decades when special education began to evolve have educators in Arab countries classified blindness and low vision as visual impairments or disabilities.

Arabic Braille was derived from English Braille more than 100 years ago. In the 1950s, a unified Arabic Braille was adopted. Following the international convention, Arabic Braille is read from left to right (Arabic language is read and written from right to left); however, abbreviations in Arabic Braille are quite different from abbreviations in English Braille.

Intellectual Disabilities

From a historical point of view, disability and special education have been associated with intellectual disabilities in particular, a trend perhaps partially explaining the negative perceptions in the Arab world of disability and special education. Historically, pervasive negative public attitudes toward persons with intellectual disabilities and low expectations of the potential and learning ability of these persons have seriously impeded the development of effective special education services for them (Yousef, 1993). Misconceptions about persons with intellectual disabilities are widespread in Arab societies (Nagata, 2007), including the general belief that these persons cannot lead full and productive lives. Consequently, the range of available placement alternatives for students with intellectual disabilities in the Arab region tends to be extremely limited. In addition, the public generally lacks information about these persons and rarely engages with them because they are generally removed from sight as a result of social stigma, perpetuating distorted concepts about this population. Out of frustration and hopelessness, most families search tirelessly for a cure for intellectual disabilities.

Attention-Deficit/Hyperactivity Disorder

Research related to attention-deficit/hyperactivity disorder (ADHD) is extremely limited. Sulaiman's study (cited in Goforth, 2011) is the only study available on ADHA among Arab Americans. This study found that 28% of Arab American youth were diagnosed with ADHD. Studies on ADHD in Arab countries are also quite rare. In a study conducted by Farah et al. (2009), epidemiological studies on ADHD in the Arab region were reviewed. Samples in studies reviewed were drawn from the general community, primary care clinical settings, and populations of traumatized children. The findings revealed that ADHD prevalence rates reported in Arab countries were similar to those in other countries. The researchers could not make comparisons among Arab studies because of the variability of methodology and instruments used.

Behavior Disorders

Empirical research on the mental health of Arab Americans is also extremely limited; however, some studies and reports in the past few years indicated that the number of Arab American people seeking mental health services has steadily increased (Meyer & Ibrahim, 2011). Compared to other minorities in the United States, Arab Americans are more vulnerable to stress, perhaps a result of their exposure to negative and inaccurate stereotypes and perceptions (Erickson & Al-Timimi, 2001; Moradi & Hasan, 2004). Moreover, many Arab Americans are recent immigrants who may experience acculturative stress (Goforth, 2011).

Research suggests that Arab Americans have relatively high rates of mental health problems. Surveys of Arab American youth suggest a high prevalence of psychological problems, such as anxiety disorder, attention-deficit/hyperactivity disorder, depressive disorder, oppositional defiant and conduct disorders, and adjustment disorders (Abu-Ras & Abu-Bader, 2009; Aprahamian, Kaplan, Windham, Sutter, & Visser, 2011; El-Sayed & Galea, 2009; Goforth, 2011; Jamil, 2002).

Amer and Hovey (2012) investigated the levels of anxiety and depression in a sample of Arab American respondents from 35 U.S. states, the majority of whom were Muslims. The results revealed that 25% of respondents reported having moderate to severe anxiety, and 50% reported having depression levels serious enough to warrant further assessment. These rates are significantly higher than those reported by normative community samples and samples of four other minority populations in the United States.

Several studies found that Arab Americans have higher rates of posttraumatic stress disorder (PTSD) compared to the general U.S. population (Rippy & Newman as cited in Goforth, 2011; Kira et al., 2014). Abu-Ras and Abu-Bader (2009) also found high rates of PTSD and depression among 350 Arab and Muslim Americans; results of their study revealed that the most important variables in predicting depression and PTSD among this population were age, education, marital status, access to support, and having children.

Arab American Families of Children with Disabilities

As in all cultures, the Arab family is impacted by the experience of disability in different ways. Hijazi (2014) noted that some Arab American parents hesitating to acknowledge that their child has a disability is a major problem in the Arab American community. Diken (2006) observed that Arab parents may consider themselves or their families as the causal agent of disability, and the child's disability may produce feelings of shame and guilt among these parents. Disability is still surrounded by ignorance, stigma, and unfavorable attitudes. This author has observed that many people in Arab societies do not like to think or talk about disabilities; however, Arab Americans are a diverse group representing various regions from the Middle East and North Africa (El-Badry, 1994). Arab people's perceptions and attitudes toward disability have shifted over the past three decades. Individuals with disabilities have become more visible in public life, special education services have continually evolved, accessibility has become more popular, parents have formed advocacy groups, and inclusive education has gained more support, among others.

Arab parents feel ashamed and humiliated by their failures or inefficiencies just as much as they feel proud and honored by their children's successes and achievements. Goforth (2011) stated, "An individual's actions or decisions not only impact the individual, but also impact other family members." Kuaider (2005) noted that when one family member experiences an illness, the entire family becomes concerned about that individual's well-being and the recovery. Disabilities negatively impact future prospects for individuals having those disabilities and their families in the Arab region. According to Donovan (2013), "negative social implications of disabilities extend to siblings, especially sisters, who tend to face diminished marriage prospects. . . . As a result, family members with disabilities might simply be kept hidden from the public" (p. 22). For this reason, Wehbi and Lakkis (cited in Donovan, 2013) found that some births of daughters with disabilities in Lebanon were never officially registered in municipal records; furthermore, this also explains why some individuals with disabilities in Arab countries are of unknown parentage.

Donovan's (2013) discussion of cultural perceptions of mental health disorders in Arab countries have important implications for understanding Arab people's explanations and reactions to disability in these countries. After reviewing and analyzing several pertinent resources, Donovan found that perceptions of mental health disorders may include some supernatural explanations, such as witchcraft and possession by spirits (called *jinn* in Arabic). Another explanation suggested by some people as a cause of mental and physical illness is the evil eye. Thus, Donovan explained, "It is customary when commenting on someone's good fortune or possessions to say *masha'allah*, or God protect you, because it indicates a lack of envy and is believed to ward off the evil eye" (p. 14). Regardless, many consider a child with a disability a gift, or a plan, or a test from God of the family's endurance and faith. Some may even consider disability a curse or the result of a family's sin or lost faith in God. Parents having such beliefs tend to seek religious counseling.

Donovan (2013) observed that seeking mental health services is generally seen as a sign of weakness in Arab countries. The same is true for special education as well as some forms of social services. This discourages many people in the Arab world from seeking assistance for their children's impairments. The stigma commonly attached to disability may also discourage some Arab American parents from evaluating their children. Instead, these parents tend to search for quick medical treatments for their children's impairments, at least in the initial stages of suspecting or diagnosing a disability.

In the Arab culture, many blame mothers for their children's disabilities. The mother, these people believe, is the one who gave birth to the child. Crabtree (2007) reported that some Arab mothers of children with disabilities worried that their husbands may divorce them and marry second wives (in Islam, men are allowed to practice polygamy, that is, they can have up to a total of four wives at the same time if certain conditions are met).

To the best of this author's knowledge, only three empirical studies have been conducted on disabilities among Arab Americans. All three of these research studies investigated issues related to families. In the next chapter, the results of these studies will be described in more detail. The first study was carried out by Kuaider (2005), who, using questionnaires and interviews, investigated the adaptation and daily routine of Arab American families of children with disabilities. Nine Arab American mothers having children with disabilities living with them participated in this study. Of these nine mothers, one was divorced, one was employed, and all had at least high school diploma and had been in the United States at least 6 years. These mothers' children were aged 5 to 18 years, had different types and degrees of disability, and received or had received special education services.

Two-thirds of the mothers revealed that they could afford the services needed by their children. Of the nine mothers, eight reported a light to moderate involvement in their children's education (e.g., volunteering, observing, attending individualized education program meetings). Mothers' perceptions of their relationships with schools varied. Most reported low to moderate home accommodations to meet the unique needs of their children. They also reported a moderate childcare and domestic workload. Fathers' participation was evaluated as little to moderate. Seven of the nine mothers received little help with childcare from either relatives or nonrelatives. Regarding domestic workload, seven mothers received little help, and two received some help from fathers, the child's siblings, or relatives.

Regarding satisfaction with mother–father relationships and sibling interactions, all mothers reported low levels of satisfaction. Families involved their children with disabilities moderately in nondisabled networks (e.g., general education classrooms, family and community activities); however, families were less involved in disability networks (e.g., parent support groups, disability groups and activities). They were moderately involved with other cultural and ethnic groups and social networks. Finally, all mothers, with only very little variability, perceived religious and spiritual practices as supportive for them in accepting and adapting to their children with disabilities.

In the second study Abadeh (2006) examined the relationships between Arab American parents of children with disabilities and their teachers. Participants in this study were limited to a random sample of 100 Arab American parents of elementary school children in one suburban school district in Michigan. A 42-item self-report instrument was used to collect data; it was translated into Arabic to accommodate parents having difficulties in reading and understanding English. A survey packet, including an informed consent form, a copy of the information letter, a copy of the survey, and a self-addressed prepaid envelope, was distributed to target parents through the school district. The results revealed that parents positively rated 9 of the 11 subscales assessed. The two subscales that reflected nonpositive attitudes of parents were parent–teacher communication and off-site communication. With the exception of face-to-face communication, no significant differences were found between U.S.-born and foreign-born Arab American parents. Abadeh also investigated whether parents' perceptions of home–school communication were influenced by parents' age, educational level, country of birth, time in the United States, and attendance in a school outside the United States. The only variable that was a significant predictor of parents' perceptions was length of time in the United States.

The third study was by Donovan (2013), who explored Arab American parents' experiences with special education and disability. More specifically, she investigated six Arab American parents' (i.e., five mothers and one father) experiences with and understanding of the American special education system, using a phenomenological qualitative approach. The study was carried out in a large city in the Midwest. Parent participants were diverse in terms of their children's gender and type of disability and the families' generation in the United States; however, all participant parents in this study were Muslim.

The results revealed that five of the six parents were referred to special education assessment by school personnel; one parent initiated referral herself. According to Donovan (2013), during the referral stage, parents experienced mixed emotions, ranging from denial to anger and from gratitude to sadness. On learning that their children had disabilities that caused them to be eligible for special education, parents reacted in different ways, including denial, fear, frustration, confusion, or anxiety.

Donovan (2013) also described parents' culture-specific concerns for their children; the most frequently cited was the potential for limited marriage prospects for persons with disabilities. She reported that the main concerns of the Arab American mothers she studied were related to the potential consequences of disability on the marriage prospects for their children as well as on their families. Donovan also noted that special education has negative connotations in the Arab culture. To Arabs and Arab Americans, the term *special education* is pejorative and offensive. Attaching the term special education to a child and his or her family may have far-reaching consequences. Because of this negative association several Arab American parents keep their children's enrollment in special education a secret.

Donovan (2013) also found that parent participants were, overall, satisfied with special education services. In particular, they were most satisfied with the specially designed instruction provided for their children. She reported that parent participants developed key supportive relationships during the special education process and that they were particularly appreciative of the school staff's genuine care and concern for their child, helpful communication, and moral support.

However, Donovan (2013) reported that half the mothers she studied also had unsupportive relationships with husbands and with school personnel, particularly Arab American teachers. Main features of unsupportive relationships with husbands were minimal or no involvement and denial of the child's disability. Negative judgment of school personnel and poor, or even painful, communication with teachers were the two main reasons for unsupportive relationships with school staff.

Parents who participated in Donovan's and Kuiader's studies mentioned previously were satisfied with some of their experiences and unsatisfied with other experiences with special education. Donovan (2013) reported the following statement by a mother:

> I was already traumatized that the kid was having problems in general. She just used all the wrong words. She didn't come at me the right way. . . . She had no heart the way she came at me.
>
> (Donovan, 2013, p. 140)

According to another Arab American mother

> When [my daughter] was three years old [the school psychologist] tested her; she tested real low. They tested her again when she was four; she tested real low. We got her to kindergarten. I begged them, "Please test my daughter. I want to get her an IEP. I want to see where my daughter is at." They never did. . . . Finally, [my daughter] was evaluated in fourth grade and identified with ADHD.
>
> (Donovan, 2013, pp. 146–147)

One mother was frustrated because the school would not inform her of the services that her child really needed. This mother was quoted by Kuaider (2005):

> They never give me information about services that will help me. I always find out the services from other parents. The school will hide the information from me and then when I bring it up if it is something they are required by law to do then they will say. "OK, OK, we can do that for you." Otherwise they don't bring it up.
>
> (p. 48)

Another mother interviewed by Kuaider (2005) thought that the school personnel did not understand her son or his family. This mother commented: "We moved from place to place, . . . so . . . we weren't happy with the school. They never understood us" (p. 49).

In contrast, some parents in Donovan's (2013) study described their experiences with special education services in the United States as both important and meaningful. These parents were satisfied with services rendered to their children. "Parents were generally satisfied with the improvement their children had demonstrated. They also appreciated the individual attention and practical assistance their children received in school and the investment the services were making into their children's futures" (Donovan, 2013, p. 162).

For instance, one mother said, "I'm very happy that [my son] is in special education because if it wasn't for special education, he would not get the help that he is getting now. It really benefited him and benefited me that my son progressed" (Donovan, 2013, p. 156). The next section in this chapter presents biographical sketch of some famous and successful Arab Americans with disabilities.

Disability in Arab Culture

Historically, persons with disabilities have been treated with massive public ignorance, shame, and marginalization in Arab societies (Al Lawati, 2011). According to Al Thani (2006), for decades, services to persons with disabilities in all Arab countries were motivated by pity and charity. In a recent book on the history of both physical and mental disabilities in the Ottoman Arab World, 1500–1800, Scalenghe (2014) pointed out that abilities or disabilities in Arab societies have always influenced individuals' status in society and impacted every aspect of their lives, including the exercise of religious practices, ability to marry, employment opportunities, and acquiring property. Although changing perceptions toward disability in Arab societies have recently been noted by some researchers (e.g., Crabtree & Williams, 2013), the remnants of cultural traditions influence contemporary practices with persons with disabilities in Arab countries. Nagata (2008) indicated that public attitudes toward people with disabilities in two Arab countries (Lebanon and Jordan) are still negative regardless of socioeconomic–demographic variables. People with disabilities are generally forgotten or invisible in Arab communities because of negative social attitudes and lack of a human rights culture (Al Thani, 2006). Commonly, families in Arab societies are ashamed to acknowledge that their child has a disability. As a result, many persons with disabilities are locked away in institutions or kept at home without receiving special education or related services (Al Lawati, 2011).

Kabbara (2014) asserted that people with disabilities in Arab countries are increasingly suffering as a result of turmoil in the region. Saif (2013) also stated that the Arab Spring, whose proponents called for better living conditions, has so far negatively impacted regional economies, especially in Tunisia, Egypt, Yemen, Libya, Syria, and some other countries. Taking the population growth into account, the postulated economic growth will be negligible, further contributing to the deterioration in standards of living (Saif, 2013). What, if any, influences the Arab Spring will have on services for people with disabilities in these countries remains to be seen.

Table 2.2 presents basic information about disability in contemporary Arab societies.

Table 2.2 Basic Information About Disability in Arab Societies

1. International estimates of the total numbers of individuals with disabilities in Arab countries range from 36,980,000 to 55,470,000.

2. Persons with disabilities in Arab region are significantly underenumerated by national authorities and suffer from marginalization.

3. Historically, services to persons with disabilities in Arab countries have been motivated by pity and charity.

4. In most Arab countries, special education appeared in the early 1980s.

5. Special education services are provided to less than 10% of persons with disabilities in the Arab region.

6. Poverty and lack of resources as well as wars and armed conflicts in several countries have contributed to a marked increase in the prevalence of disabilities, and they have prevented governments from providing appropriate special education services.

7. Kinship marriage, which is a negative sociocultural factor in inherited disabilities, still prevails in the Arab region.

8. Overall, persons with disabilities (especially women and those with intellectual disabilities) are invisible in Arab societies because of negative social attitudes and the lack of a human rights culture.

(Continued)

Table 2.2 (Continued)

9. Because of the stigma attached to people with disabilities in the Arab region, most Arab families tend to be ashamed of their children with diagnosed disabilities.

10. The special education system in Arab countries remains, to a large extent, institution based instead of community oriented; very limited inclusive education programs have been implemented.

11. Special education budgets are very limited.

12. A serious lack of family involvement characterizes special education programs.

13. Some disability categories (e.g., behavior disorders and speech and language disorders) remain neglected.

14. Teacher training in special education is still relatively scarce in most Arab countries.

15. Most Arab countries have yet to meet some basic challenges with regard to the rights of persons with disabilities, public awareness, gathering and using information and statistics on disability, and creating accessible physical environments.

16. Inclusion is not rights based nor does it occur in response to equalization initiatives; instead, it is the only alternative to isolation and marginalization.

17. Identification and assessment of students with disabilities still represent a major challenge.

18. Appropriate curricula to respond to individual needs of children with disabilities are lacking.

19. A major challenge facing Arab countries regards education for young children and adults with disabilities.

20. Most Arab countries recently formulated special education policies and legislation; however, a lack of policy enforcing mechanisms remains an issue.

Sources: (Alhadidi & Alkhateeb, 2015; AlQuraini, 2014; ESCWA & LAS, 2014).

Definitions of Disability

No single Arab definition or classification system for disabilities is available. In no Arab country has a consensus on definitions of disabilities been adopted by relevant authorities. Definitions adopted in disability laws in Arab countries are similar but generally tend to be vague and too broad. These laws define people with disabilities but do not include types of disabilities. With the exception of disability laws in Qatar and Yemen, these laws also fail to mention special education; instead, they focus on care and rehabilitation. Arab population censuses, however, classify disabilities into five categories: motor disabilities, blindness, deafness, intellectual disability, and multiple disabilities.

Disability in Arab countries has commonly been defined as a physical, mental, or psychological condition that limits a person's activities. For example, the 2007 law for the rights of people with disabilities in Jordan, similar to disability laws in Arab countries, defines a person with disability as follows:

> A person with a disability is a person having a total or partial impairment in any of the senses or physical, psychological or intellectual abilities, to an extent that limits his/her capacity for learning or habilitation or working and renders him/her unable to meet his ordinary life requirements under the same conditions of the non-disabled people.
>
> (Higher Council for Persons with Disabilities; 2007, p. 1)

By contrast, definitions and categories of disabilities used and recognized in professional and academic circles, such as universities, special education departments, and organizations, are more consistent with internationally adopted definitions. By and large, these definitions and classifications are translations into Arabic definitions used in international disability and special education literature.

Prevalence of Disability

Prior to 1980, no data were available about disability statistics in the Arab region. In the 1980s, few Arab countries (e.g., Jordan, Yemen) collected prevalence data on disability through surveys with a focus on four categories: blindness, deafness, intellectual impairment, and orthopedic impairments (amputation and paralysis). Then in the 1990s and later, information about disabilities was obtained through population censuses in many Arab countries. Because population censuses are often based on more narrow interpretations of disability, they produce lower prevalence rates that only reflect more severe impairments (ESCWA & LAS, 2014). In addition, social stigma is known to discourage people from reporting disabilities, and this may help to explain the remarkably low disability prevalence rates that range from 0.4% in Qatar to 4.9% in the Sudan (ESCWA & LAS, 2014). Al Thani (2006) commented on the low rates of disability prevalence reported by Arab countries as follows: "In many ways, this is akin to 'being in denial': It is easier to deny the existence of a condition than to have to deal with it" (p. 7).

Like most developing countries, Arab countries report disability prevalence rates that focus on a subpopulation of persons with more severe disabilities. No information is obtained on the following disability categories: learning disabilities, behavior disorders, autism spectrum disorders, and speech–language impairments. Censuses also provide information on blindness, deafness, and more severe levels of intellectual impairments, but little or no information is obtained on partial vision, hard of hearing, and mild degrees of intellectual disabilities.

The exact number of people with disabilities in the Arab region is unknown. In a recently published report, however, Arab countries reported prevalence of disability rates ranging from 0.4% to 4.9% of the

Table 2.3 Estimated Numbers of People with Disabilities in Arab Countries According to National and International Estimates

Country	Total Population (millions)*	National Estimates**	International Estimates***	
			Low estimate (10%)	High estimate (15%)
Algeria	39.2	980,000 (2.5%)	3,920,000	5,880,000
Bahrain	1.3	37,700 (2.9%)	130,000	195,000
Comoros	0.7	–	70,000	105,000
Djibouti	0.9	–	90,000	135,000
Egypt	82.1	5,747,000 (0.7%)	8,210,000	1,231,500
Iraq	33.4	935,200 (2.8%)	3,340,000	5,010,000
Jordan	6.5	123,500 (1.9%)	650,000	975,000
Kuwait	3.4	37,400 (1.1%)	340,000	510,000
Lebanon	4.5	90,000 (2.0%)	450,000	675,000
Libya	6.2	179,800 (2.9%)	620,000	930,000
Mauritania	3.9	–	390,000	585,000
Morocco	33.0	759,000 (2.3%)	3,300,000	4,950,000
Oman	3.6	82,800 (3.2%)	360,000	540,000
Qatar	2.2	8,800 (0.4%)	220,000	330,000
Saudi Arabia	28.8	230,400 (0.8%)	1,500,000	4,320,000
Somalia	10.5	–	3,800,000	1,575,000
Sudan	38.0	1,862,000 (4.9%)	3,800,000	5,700,000
Syria	22.8	319,200 (1.4%)	2,280,000	3,420,000
Tunisia	10.9	141,700 (1.3%)	1,900,000	1,635,000
UAE	9.3	74,400 (0.8%)	930,000	1,395,000
West Bank and Gaza	4.2	193,200 (4.6%)	420,000	630,000
Yemen	24.4	463,600 (1.9%)	2,440,000	3,660,000
Total	369.8	12,265,700	36,980,000	55,470,000

* World Bank (2014)
** ESCWA and LAS (2014)
*** Mont (2007); WHO (2012)

population (ESCWA & LAS, 2014), making the Arab population with disabilities about 12.3 million. Disability prevalence in Arab countries may be even higher than in other regions, given the widespread occurrence of risk factors, including consanguinity, poverty, communicable diseases, armed conflict, poor health care, poor nutrition, and illiteracy (Gharaibeh, 2009; Mont, 2007). In fact, calculations by international organizations have estimated disability prevalence rates in developing countries, including Arab countries, at 10%–15% of the total population (Mont, 2007; World Health Organization, 2011). Based upon these international calculations, the total number of people with disabilities in Arab countries can be estimated at roughly between 37 million to 55 million persons (see Table 2.3). In light of this information, the ESCWA and LAS (2014) concluded that existing disability prevalence rates in Arab countries must be viewed with skepticism.

Causes of Disabilities

With the exception of studies conducted by medical researchers on the etiologies and risk factors of chronic illnesses and some types of impairments (e.g., blindness, neuropsychiatric disorders, cardiovascular diseases, endocrine disorders, pulmonary diseases, and musculoskeletal problems), information about the causes of disabilities in Arab countries is scant. Although experts have no reason to believe that the causes of disability in Arab societies are radically different from the rest of the world, some features may contribute to higher than normal prevalence rates of disability in the Arab region (Gharaibeh, 2009). Among risk factors of special concern in Arab countries are genetic and congenital factors.

Research has shown that Arab countries have one of the highest rates of genetic diseases in the world (Center for Arab Genomic Studies, 2012; Elass, 2009; Tadmouri, 2013). Available evidence suggests that these disorders are responsible for a major proportion of physical and intellectual disabilities in Arab countries (Al-Ghazali, Hamamy, & Al-Arrayad, 2006; Teebi & Farag, 1997). Congenital malformations caused by recessive genes and metabolic disorders are the most common disorders throughout the Arab world (Al-Ghazali et al., 2006). Also common are thalassemia, diabetes, sickle cell disorder, heart disease, Down syndrome, muscular dystrophy, and phenylketonuria (Teebi & Farag, 1997).

High rates of consanguinity (marriage between relatives) represent a major risk factor, and on average, it exceeds 30% of marriages in the Arab world (Gharaibeh, 2009). In addition, large family size and advanced maternal and paternal age are primary reasons for the higher prevalence of genetic disorders in the Arab world. Genetic diseases may be responsible for up to two-thirds of both childhood deafness and blindness in Arab societies (Gharaibeh, 2009).

Chronic and communicable diseases, such as cardiovascular diseases, chronic respiratory conditions, trachoma, measles, meningitis, otitis media, tuberculosis, and malaria remain prevalent in some parts of the Arab world (Abdul-Haq, 2008). Such diseases may be causative factors in developmental disabilities; however, Mokdad et al. (2014) recently found that disability caused by communicable, newborn, nutritional, and maternal disorders has decreased in the Arab region since 1990. Mineral and vitamin deficiencies, which may result in physical and intellectual impairments if not treated, are also common in many Arab countries (Abdul-Haq, 2008). Poverty can cause disability through malnutrition, poor health care, and poor living conditions. According to Gharaibeh (2009), poverty may be a main reason for preventable disability across many Arab countries.

Arab people have been exhausted by prolonged upheavals besetting the region. For years, turmoil in the Arab region has occupied a prominent place in the headlines. Wars and unrest in Syria, Iraq, Libya, Somalia, and the Palestinian Territories are just few examples. Armed conflict is among the preventable causes of disabilities. Landmines and random explosions may result in death as well as large numbers of physical or sensory disabilities. Wars and armed conflicts also produce invisible psychosocial disabilities resulting from trauma. For every child killed in armed violence, 100 children are left with permanent, life-long disabilities (Office of the U. N. Special Rapporteur on Disability, 2007). Furthermore, the protection and safety of people with disabilities in armed conflicts are very commonly neglected. Immunization practices may be suspended, and access to health and rehabilitation services may become limited.

Road traffic accidents, which are a major cause of death and disability worldwide, are very high in Arab countries compared to other regions of the world (Semlali, 2013). Reasons include poor transportation infrastructure and poor planning and organization of traffic flow, driver behavior, and poor enforcement of traffic laws resulting in a disregard for safety (Gharaibeh, 2009).

Work-related injuries, which may cause disabilities among workers, are also high in the Arab region (Habib, 2007). These injuries are believed to be the result of such factors as lack of occupational safety, poor management systems, and poor supervision and enforcement of regulations (Abdul-Haq, 2008). Finally, underdevelopment, the lack of resources in some countries, pockets of high illiteracy rates, and the less-than-adequate response by governments have also had an impact on the prevalence of disability (Al-Thani, 2006).

Stigma

Arab societies generally regard disability as a stigmatizing condition that affects the entire family (Crabtree, 2007). The term *disability* is considered by many to be an insult. Gharaibeh (2009) noted, "The Arabic words used to describe disabilities of different sorts are all stigmatizing, but some are more stigmatizing than others. The Arabic word commonly used for disability in children . . . literally means handicap, hindrance, cause for delay" (p. 70). The words used to describe males as well as females with a disability "are pejorative words meaning 'backward,' 'retarded,' 'delayed,' 'unable to keep up,' or 'left behind'" (Gharaibeh, 2009, p. 71). However, overgeneralizations should be avoided because research indicates Arab families may show positive attitudes toward children with disabilities based on religious parity as well as parental love and affection (Crabtree, 2007).

In Arab societies, intellectual disabilities are more stigmatizing than physical or sensory disabilities. Gender plays a role in disability stigma: females are generally subjected to more disability stigma than males, especially in conservative parts of the Arab world. Gharaibeh (2009) stated that women face double discrimination, first for being a female and second for having a disability.

Al Thani (2006) painted a bleak picture about the situation of women with disabilities in Arab countries. She wrote:

> As women, they are segregated from male society, but as women with disabilities they are also isolated from the lives of other women. They are, for all intents and purposes, invisible; their issues receive little, or no, consideration; and there are very few programs that target them specifically.
>
> (p. 7)

Research conducted by Crabtree (2007) indicated that disability in sons was more disappointing to the Arab parents she studied than in daughters. This is understandable given that sons in Arab societies are presumed to have a more important function for the family, such as support for parents once they have aged, greater economic net utility, and the responsibility for carrying on the family name. This issue, however, like most other issues related to disability in Arab societies, needs to be researched more thoroughly.

In rural and nomadic segments of the Arab population, where the communal identity of the extended family and tribe are most important, persons with disabilities may be at a distinct disadvantage. In these societies, "People with disabilities are made to feel, explicitly or implicitly, that they are a liability. Negative attitudes toward a child with disability are fueled by holding him or her accountable for the adversity suffered by relatives" (Gharaibeh, 2009, pp. 71–72).

However, stigma attached to disability is not unique to Arab culture. Potentially stigmatizing public beliefs about the causes of disability are common among different cultures (Scior, Addai-Davies, Kenyon, & Sheridan, 2013). For example, Westbrook, Legge, and Pennay (1993) reported that the relative degree of stigma attached to disability was similar across six different ethnic communities. In Asian cultures, families of children with disabilities tend to rely on support from family and friends and may be reluctant to seek formal help because of the social stigma associated with disability. Parents may believe it is inappropriate to accept help from others (Baker, Miller, Dang, Yaangh, & Hansen, 2010). Also, a child with a disability may affect the marriage prospects of family members (Canadian Pediatric Society, 2016). In these cultures, a child's disability may be perceived as caused by possession by spirits, magic, or punishment for sins committed by the mother or individual (Canadian Pediatric Society, 2016; Hatton, Akram, Robertson, Shah, & Emerson, 2003). The stigma attached to disability in these cultures can result in parents hiding their children with disabilities from the community and becoming socially isolated (McGrother, Bhaumik, Thorp, Watson, & Taub, 2002). Families in some Asian and African cultures seek out the help of health and spiritual care providers. Families in these cultures may also seek treatment from *traditional* healers and providers of complementary and alternative medicine (Baker et al., 2010). Black and minority ethnic groups in south London were reported to believe that disability was a punishment for past sins (Hubert, 2006). Ravindran and Myers (2012) noted that a child's disability is viewed as a consequence of the mother's sins in Puerto Rico, as a punishment for sins committed by the child or parent in a past life in India, as a consequence of curse by an "evil eye" in some Latin American cultures, and as a result of negative forces in China. In the United States and other Western countries, there have been significant changes during the past five decades in attitudes toward people with disabilities and in the way these people are treated in school and other settings. However, while that attitudes toward people with disabilities have improved, there is evidence that negative attitudes persist (Aaberg, 2012; Ferrara, Burns, & Mills, 2015; National Disability Authority, 2010; Current attitudes towards disabled people, 2014). As a result, most of the isolated institutions have been replaced with community integration (U.S. Department of Education, 2008).

Special Education and Related Services

Special education in Arab countries emerged and, to a very large extent, remains institution based instead of community oriented. Special segregated centers and institutions for individuals with intellectual disabilities, hearing impairments, visual impairments, and physical disabilities were initially established in the 1960s in some Arab countries. Services in these facilities were based on compassion and charity work. Until the 1970s, such facilities expanded and were founded by private and volunteer sectors. In that era, only on-the-job training for personnel was implemented (Yousef, 1993). In the early 1980s, some Arab universities and community colleges offered diploma programs in special education. Shortly thereafter, undergraduate and graduate programs in this area were introduced. This development was accompanied by increasing teacher training, research, tests, publications, seminars, and conferences related to disability. In addition, surveys of disability prevalence rates emerged in few Arab countries in the 1980s. Special education departments were established by ministries of education in some countries, and new approaches to special education provision (e.g., resource rooms, self-contained classes) evolved. These services were geared almost entirely to school-age students with blindness, deafness, physical disabilities, and intellectual disabilities. In the 1990s, special education services for students with learning disabilities and autism finally appeared. Students with other disabilities (e.g., speech and language disorders and behavior disorders) remained generally unserved (Alhadidi & Alkhateeb, in press).

After 1990, most Arab countries enacted laws for the "care and rehabilitation" of people with disabilities and established more special education centers and schools. Influenced by international trends toward inclusive education, Arab countries reformulated their educational policies to promote the inclusion of an increasing number of students with mild disabilities into mainstream schools (Gaad, 2010). More recently, the majority of Arab countries ratified the U.N. Convention on the Rights of people with disabilities of 2006; however, the ESCWA and LAS (2014) noted that "While laws and regulations on education for persons with disabilities are widespread in the Arab region, available data suggest that these frameworks have limited impact on the ground" (p. 18).

In a recent article, Alhadidi and Alkhateeb (2015) discussed major challenges currently facing Arab countries in special education. A major challenge identified by these authors is the lack of access to services. Most people with disabilities in Arab countries encounter difficulties accessing special education services. These services reach only a very small percentage of students with disabilities. Parents in the Arab region who suspect or have just learned that their child has a disability commonly experience great difficulties in finding potential service providers. In addition to few choices, service providers' names, contact information, and types and quality of services offered are not easily accessible. Appropriate referral and diagnostic services that can help are not always available. Guides, handbooks, manuals, or pamphlets that might assist parents in navigating local, national, or regional special education providers are very rare; therefore, parents may seek the help of relatives, friends, or anyone else in searching for services for their children.

A second challenge is the wide gap that exists between announced special education policies in Arab countries and the actual situation on the ground. A third challenge relates to the tremendous barriers encountered in implementing effective inclusive education. As Peters (2009) noted: "Few of the children [with disabilities] have access to education, and for the few that do, the only integrated programs are nascent, and small in scope within a system that remains largely segregated between general and special education" (p. 28). Furthermore, serious shortcomings still permeate most aspects of special education teacher training at both the preservice and inservice levels. Finally, very little attention is given in Arab countries to partnerships with families and parents of children with disabilities.

The availability and adequacy of related services (e.g., speech–language pathology services, physical and occupational therapy, interpreting services, rehabilitation counseling, adapted physical education, etc.) vary widely across disciplines and countries in the Arab region. For instance, interpreting services, medical and nursing services, and social work services have been provided in most Arab countries for many years. Conversely, rehabilitation counseling, adapted physical education, and recreational therapy continue to be uncommon in many Arab countries.

Although the Arab region continues to lag behind so much of the world in information technology, some Arab countries have gained experience in using and developing assistive technology (AT) to help Arab individuals with disabilities. In particular, the Arab Gulf countries (such as Qatar, Saudi Arabia, and the United Arab Emirates) have had effective impact on these fields in the region. The Qatar Assistive Technology Center, established in 2010, is one example. This center provides information, development, and support to people with disabilities, utilizing AT across the Gulf and the Middle East region. It carries out public awareness activities, provides technologies for users, conducts assessments, and implements professional development training programs (MADA Qatar Assistive Technology Center, 2012). Most Arab countries also have adequate facilities for prosthetic and orthotic devices. Many prosthetic and orthotic centers have opened in countries like Saudi Arabia, Palestine, Lebanon, Iraq, Yemen, Egypt, and Syria. In addition, many colleges offer undergraduate programs in orthotics and prosthetics in countries such as Jordan, Saudi Arabia, Iraq, Oman, and Egypt. Long-term health care has been provided in hospitals and other health care facilities in most Arab countries for decades. Many of these facilities provided services for patients with mental health disorders and physical disabilities (Kronfol, 2012). Major weaknesses of these services include the following: (a) lack of awareness of the specific needs of these populations, (b) hurdles of access to services resulting from mobility restrictions, (c) limited health literacy, and (d) bureaucratic and fragmented service provision.

Jordan and Egypt have been pioneers in offering Bachelor of Science programs in allied health sciences in the Arab region. In Jordan, several public and private universities currently offer undergraduate programs in physical therapy, occupational therapy, prosthetics and assistive devices, and hearing and speech sciences. Among these are the University of Jordan, Hashemite University, and Jordan University of Science and Technology. In Egypt, undergraduate programs in these disciplines are offered by many universities, including Cairo University, Misr University, and October 6 University.

Dukmak (2009) reported shortages in rehabilitation services in the UAE for individuals with disabilities, which were the result of the absence of specific policies and by deficits in administrative system rather than lack of financial resources. Problems in accessing rehabilitation services were related to providers of services and parents' lack of awareness of the potential benefits of rehabilitation services.

There are very few studies on related services for students with disabilities in the Arab region. No study has been carried out in such a way that the adequacy of related services could be analyzed. Nonetheless, studies on related services in Saudi Arabia indicated the availability of transportation, counseling, social work, and school health services. However, serious shortages were reported in speech and language pathology, rehabilitation counseling, physical therapy, and occupational therapy services (Alquraini, 2010).

Institution-based vocational rehabilitation programs for persons with disabilities in Arab countries are generally outdated. Whether in terms of vocational assessment and evaluation, vocational training, career counseling, job search, or job accommodation, these programs, if available at all, are of a very low quality. They stereotype the capabilities of persons with disabilities and offer programs that lag behind contemporary rehabilitation concepts and practices. According to a report by Economic and Social Commission for Western Asia (2014),

> High disparities in economic activity and employment rates can be found when comparing data on persons with disabilities with data on total populations. . . . In almost all countries where data is readily available, persons with disabilities report substantially lower levels of employment than their peers without disabilities. In some cases, employment rates for persons with disabilities are half or even one third that of the total population.
>
> (p. 15)

In addition to institution-based rehabilitation, nongovernmental organizations (NGOs) in Arab countries implement community-based rehabilitation (CBR) with technical assistance from WHO, ILO, and UNESCO (Japan International Cooperation Agency, 2002). Examples of countries with CBR are Jordan, Syria, Egypt, Iraq, Lebanon, Morocco, Palestine, Sudan, and Yemen.

Still, rehabilitation services in Arab countries remain very limited and of modest quality. According to a World Bank (2005) report, rehabilitation services in many Arab countries reach an average of 5% to 20% of target populations. In some countries, rehabilitation services are provided only for persons with physical impairments. In most other countries, these services are also provided for individuals with sensory impairments and intellectual disabilities.

Prominent Arab Americans with Disabilities

This section introduces two famous Arab American individuals with disabilities: Lily Bandak and Maysoon Zayid. It also introduces three Arab Americans who challenged their disabilities: Rabih Dow, Khodr Farhat, and Mona Ramouni.

Lily Bandak

Lily Bandak is a world-famous Arab American photographer and advocate. Born in Amman, Jordan, to a Palestinian family from Bethlehem, she has lived in the United States since 1960, residing in Newark, Delaware. She was educated at the Academie De La Grande Chaumier in Paris, the Philadelphia College of Art, the University of Delaware, and the Antonelli College of Photography. She was the personal photographer of Mrs. Anwar Sadat and the King and Queen of Jordan. In 1978, Bandak was invited by the Egyptian government to document Egyptian culture by photographing its people and monuments. She also photographed Yasser Arafat and Nazik Hariri (widow of former Lebanese Prime Minister Rafik Hariri). She has also exhibited at the California Museum of Science and Industry, the World Trade Center in New York City, at the Capital Rotunda in Washington DC, Los Angeles, and at the Paralympic Games in Atlanta, Georgia. She has done many other exhibitions around the world. Her work is part of the permanent collection at the White House (Bandak, n.d.).

In 1983, she launched a photo-journalism department at Yarmouk University in Jordan and began to teach photography. A year later, Bandak was diagnosed with multiple sclerosis and stopped working as a result of her physical disability. An assistive technology center helped her design a camera mount to be attached to her wheelchair, enabling her to return to work. In 1994, she founded the Bandak Foundation to encourage people with disabilities to enter the workforce and integrate into society. Bandak travels across the Middle East and the United States promoting independence for people with multiple sclerosis (Bandak, n.d.).

In 2009, Bandak established Assistive Technology Makes Independence Accessible (ATMIA), a nonprofit organization whose mission is to raise awareness about the technology available to people living with disabilities in the Middle East and North Africa. Through adapted programs and services, ATMIA seeks to improve the quality of life of people with disabilities at school, work, and home (Bandak, 2012).

In March, 2012 Bandak's house caught fire, and she was carried from her burning home with the help of neighbors and a San Diego police officer. The fire destroyed her photographs and negatives along with a van outfitted for her specialized wheelchair (Gonzales & Stickney, 2012). In a recent interview with *Ability Magazine* (2014), Bandak renewed her commitment to enable people in Arab countries to use assistive technologies. She told *Ability Magazine*, "I would like to bring people to learn about assistive technology so they could go back to their countries and help people with disabilities."

Maysoon Zayid

Maysoon Zayid is an Arab American actress, comedian, writer, and activist born with cerebral palsy. Of Palestinian descent and born in New Jersey in 1974, she is considered one of America's first female Muslim comedians. She performs standup comedy nationwide as well as overseas (Institute for Middle East Understanding, 2006). In an inspiring TED talk, she said: "I got 99 problems, and palsy is just one."

Zayid began her career as an actor after earning an undergraduate degree in acting from Arizona State University by appearing on a popular soap opera. She was a full-time on-air contributor with Keith Olbermann and has most recently appeared on the *Melissa Harris-Perry Show* and *Huffington Post Live*. Zayid then turned to standup, appearing at New York's top clubs. She is known for her appearance in two motion pictures, *You Don't Mess with the Zohan* (2008) and *The Muslims Are Coming!* (2013), and a British television series titled *The Cradle of Comedy* (2012).

Along with comedian Dean Obeidallah, she founded the New York Arab-American Comedy Festival in 2003. Maysoon jokes about her family, global culture, and her life with cerebral palsy. TED (2014) made this comment about Zayid:

> Listening to the Palestinian-American combating stereotypes of Islam and Arabs with humor, touching on American political affairs, verbally frying male-dominated Hollywood, or addressing the question of

Palestine and Israel, it's hard to get a handle on her, and some come away asking, "What's the deal with this Maysoon Zayid?"

Zayid spends 3 months a year in the Palestinian territories, running an arts program for children with disabilities and orphaned children in refugee camps. She helps them use art to deal with trauma and bridge the gap between disabled and nondisabled children. Most of the funding for the camps comes from her comedy work (Institute for Middle East Understanding, 2006).

In addition to the two pioneering women introduced previously, many more Arab Americans with disabilities have challenged disability and become successful. The success stories of three more Arab Americans, all of whom have blindness, follow.

Rabih Dow

Born in Lebanon, Rabih Dow lost his eyesight and left hand at age 16 in an explosion in 1982 during the Lebanese civil war. Searching for medical treatment, he traveled to Europe and later to the United States, where he has since resided. Currently, Dow is director of rehabilitation services and international training and fencing coach at the Carroll Center for the Blind in Newton, Massachusetts (Arab American News, 2013).

An artist, a fencing coach, and a translator of Arabic poetry, Dow has presented at national and international universities and professional conferences on the issue of disability and rehabilitation. He received the Excellence and Great Achievements Award for his work in rehabilitation and disability from the Lebanese American Heritage Club in 2013 (Arab American News, 2013). Dow's insight, empathy, and confidence are inspirational to Carroll Center clients learning to navigate the world without vision. He said, "We remove blindness as a person's defining characteristic because it is not" (Boston College Alumni and Parents, 2014).

Khodr Farhat

Khodr Farhat is an Arab American of Lebanese decent living in Dearborn, Michigan. He was born with retinitis pigmentosa (RP), an inherited degenerative eye disease in which the retina progressively degenerates, causing severe vision impairment and often blindness. According to Partain (n.d.), Farhat has faced numerous struggles related to immigration, language, and acculturation to American society; however, "these experiences have shaped him to become very talented, energetic, and motivated as he encourages others through his involvement" (Partain, n.d.). The Exchange Club of Lincoln

Park, Michigan, honored Farhat as the Youth of January 2012 and the Youth of the Year 2012.

Currently, Farhat is working on his undergraduate degree in special education at Henry Ford College. He also volunteers at the Detroit Medical Center, Carr Elementary School in Lincoln Park, and the Wayne County Regional Library for the Blind and Physically Handicapped. His voluntary work focuses on teaching Braille reading and writing and orientation and mobility. In addition, he helps these individuals acquire skills needed to operate and access various technology equipment such as, iPhones, iPads, and computers (Oliver, 2014). He also actively participates in education the public about people with disabilities through speeches in front of community organizations and youth clubs.

Mona Ramouni

Mona Ramouni is a young Arab American woman of Jordanian descent, pursuing graduate studies in rehabilitation counseling at Michigan State University in 2011. She has blindness and works as an editor of Braille books. Ramouni chose to purchase a miniature guide horse instead of a guide dog (Leubsdorf, 2009) in part because miniature horses live much longer than dogs; but she had two more reasons for preferring a guide horse. First, she practices the Islamic faith, whose adherents believe that dog saliva is unclean; and second, she describes herself as a horse person. Mona loves her guide horse, Cali. In 2011, Cali was 5 years old and stood 30 inches tall, the size of a Newfoundland dog (Manning, 2011).

In an interview with Wolcott (2011), Ramouni said, "Sometimes sitting in public with Cali, I will just hug her and kiss her. I just can't even explain to you how much I love her. She's so loyal. I can't imagine going and getting another horse." Ramouni, however, says that it is common for people to ask her a lot of questions and that some of her experiences have been unpleasant. The new Americans with Disabilities Act guidelines allow individuals with blindness to use miniature horses and permit trained guide horses to be granted the same access rights as those granted to guide dogs. She had an influence in this regard (Manning, 2011). Ramouni's ultimate goal is to start a foundation for people with disabilities who would like to have a guide horse. She told Wolcott (2011) that she was eager to share this wonderful bond with others in similar positions.

Other Arab American people with disabilities or their parents have made significant achievements. It is the hope of the author that these people's biographies or autobiographies will be written and circulated, especially among Arab American communities in the United States.

References

Aaberg, V. A. (2012). A path to greater inclusivity through understanding implicit attitudes toward disability. *Journal of Nursing Education, 51*(9), 505–510.

Abadeh, H. (2006). *Perceptions of Arab American parents with children with special needs regarding home–school communications* (Doctoral dissertation). Retrieved from ProQuest Dissertations and Theses database. (UMI No. 304972765).

Abdul-Haq, A. K. (2008). Disability. In L. S. Naser & A. K. Abdul-Haq (Eds.), *Caring for Arab patients* (pp. 117–123). Oxon, UK: Radcliffe Publishing.

Abdulrahim, S., & Baker, W. (2009). Differences in self-rated health by immigrant status and language preference among Arab Americans in the Detroit metropolitan area. *Social Science and Medicine, 68*(12), 2097–2103.

Ability Magazine. (2014). Lily Bandak: A clear focus. Retrieved from www.ability-magazine.com/past.html

Abraham, N. (1995). Arab Americans. In R. J. Vecoli, J. Galens, A. Sheets, & R. V. Young (Eds.), *Gale encyclopedia of multicultural America* (Vol. 1, pp. 84–98). New York, NY: Gale Research.

Abudabbeh, N. (2005). Arab families: An overview. In M. McGoldrick, J. Giordano, & N. Garcia-Preto (Eds.), *Ethnicity and family therapy* (3rd ed., pp. 423–436). New York, NY: Guilford Press.

Abu-Ras, W., & Abu-Bader, S. H. (2009). Risk factors for depression and posttraumatic stress disorder (PTSD): The case of Arab and Muslim Americans post-9/11. *Journal of Immigrant and Refugee Studies, 7*(4), 393–418.

Al-Fityani, K., & Padden, K. (2010). *A lexical comparison of sign languages in the Arab world.* Retrieved from www.editora-arara-azul.com.br/ebooks/catalogo/1.pdf

Al-Ghazali, L., Hamamy, H., & Al-Arrayad, S. (2006). Genetic disorders in the Arab world. *The BMJ.* Retrieved from www.bmj.com/cgi/content/full/ 333/7573/831

Alhadidi, M. S., & Alkhateeb, J. M. (2015). Special education in Arab countries: Current challenges. *International Journal of Disability, Development, and Education, 62*(5), 518–530.

AlHajal, K. (2009). *Autism school gives hope to immigrant families.* Retrieved from www.arabamericannews.com/news/news/id_2323

Al Lawati, S. (2011). Mentally disabled children in the Middle East and their integration into society. *Middle East Health.* Retrieved from www.middleeasthealthmag.com/cgi-bin/index.cgi?http://www.middleeasthealthmag.com/jul2011/feature5.htm

Alquraini, T. A. (2010). Special education in Saudi Arabia: Challenges, perspectives, future possibilities. *International Journal of Special Education, 25*(3), 139–147.

Alquraini, T. A. (2014). Special education today in the Kingdom of Saudi Arabia. In A. F. Rotatori, J. P. Bakken, S. Burkhardt, F. E. Obiakor, & U. Sharma (Eds.), *Special education international perspectives: Practices across the globe (Advances in special education)* (Vol. 28, pp. 505–528). Bradford, UK: Emerald Group.

Al Thani, H. (2006). Disability in the Arab region: Current situation and prospects. *Journal for Disability and International Development, 3*, 4–9. Retrieved from www.iiz-dvv.de/index.php?article_id=137&clang=1

Amer, M. M., & Hovey, J. D. (2012). Anxiety and depression in a post-September 11 sample of Arabs in the USA. *Social Psychiatry and Psychiatric Epidemiology, 47*(3), 409–418.

Aprahamian, M., Kaplan, D. M., Windham, A. M., Sutter, J. A., & Visser, J. (2011). The relationship between acculturation and mental health of Arab Americans. *Journal of Mental Health Counseling, 33*(1). Retrieved from www.readperiodi cals.com/201101/ 2263929001.html

Arab American Institute. (2012). *Demographics.* Retrieved from www.aaiusa.org/ pages/ demographics

Arab American News. (2013). *Visually impaired Arab American to be honored for work in rehabilitation and disability.* Retrieved from www.arabamericannews. com/ news/news/id_6582

Baker, D. L., Miller, E., Dang, M. T., Yaangh, C. S., & Hansen, R. L. (2010). Developing culturally responsive approaches with Southeast Asian American families experiencing developmental disabilities. *Pediatrics, 126*(Suppl 3), S146–S150.

Bandak, L. (2012). *Assistive Technology Makes Independence Accessible* (ATMIA). Retrieved from lilybandak.com

Bandak, L. (n.d.). *Arab world photography.* Retrieved from http://udel.edu/~bandak/ arabworldphotography/gallery.html

Bener, A., ElHakeem, A. A., & Abdulhadi, K. (2005). Is there any association between consanguinity and hearing loss? *International Journal of Pediatric Otorhinolaryngology, 69*(3), 327–333.

Boston College Alumni and Parents. (2014). *Rabih Dow '91.* Retrieved from www. bc.edu/alumni/news/news . . ./rabih_dow_profile.html

Brault, M. W. (2012). Americans with disabilities: 2010. *Household Economic Studies, Current Population Reports.* Retrieved from www.census.gov/prod/2012pubs/ p70–131.pdf

Campbell-Wilson, F. (2012). Middle East and Arab American cultures. In D. E. Battle (Ed.), *Communication disorders in multicultural and international populations* (4th ed., pp. 61–75). St. Louis, MO: Mosby.

Canadian Pediatric Society. (2016). *Developmental disability across cultures.* Retrieved from www.kidsnewtocanada.ca/mental-health/developmental-disability

Center for Arab Genomic Studies. (2012). *Genetic disorders in the Arab world.* Retrieved from www.cags.org.ae

Crabtree, S. A. (2007). Culture, gender, and the influence of social change amongst Emirati families in the United Arab Emirates. *Journal of Comparative Family Studies, 38*, 575–587.

Crabtree, S., & Williams, R. (2013). Ethical implications for research into inclusive education in Arab societies: Reflections on the politicization of the personalized research experience. *International Social Work, 56*(2), 148–161.

Current attitudes towards disabled people. (2014). *Scope.* Retrieved from www. scope.org.uk/. . ./Current-attitudes-towards-disabled

Dallo, F. J., Al Snih, S., & Ajrouch, K. J. (2009). Prevalence of disability among US and foreign-born Arab Americans: Results from the 2000 US Census. *Gerontology, 55*(2), 153–161.

Diken, I. H. (2006). An overview of parental perceptions in cross-cultural groups on disability. *Childhood Education, 82*(4), 236–240.

Donovan, E. (2013). *A phenomenological exploration of Arab American parents' experiences with the special education process* (Doctoral dissertation). Retrieved from https://etd.ohiolink.edu/ap:0:0:APPLICATION_PROCESS=DOWNLOAD_ETD_SUB_DOC_ACCNUM:::F1501_ID:kent1372583897, inline

Dukmak, S. (2009). Rehabilitation services in the United Arab Emirates as perceived by parents of children with disabilities. *The Journal of Rehabilitation, 75*(4), 27–34.

Economic and Social Commission for Western Asia and League of Arab States. (2014). *Disability in the Arab region: An overview.* Retrieved from www.escwa.un.org/divisions/div_editor/Download.asp?table_name=divisions_other&field_name=ID&FileID=1658

Elass, R. (2009). *Arabs bear brunt of gene disorders.* Retrieved from www.thenational.ae/news/uae-news/arabs-bear-brunt-of-gene-disorders

El-Badry, S. (1994). The Arab-Americans. *American Demographics, 75*(1), 22–30.

El-Sayed, A. M., & Galea, S. (2009). The health of Arab-Americans living in the United States: A systematic review of the literature. *BMC Public Health, 9*, 272–280.

El-Sayed, A. M., Tracy, M., Scarborough, P., & Galea, S. (2011). Ethnic inequalities in mortality: The case of Arab Americans. *PLOS One, 6*(12). Retrieved from www.ncbi.nlm.nih.gov

Erickson, C. D., & Al-Timimi, N. R. (2001). Providing mental health services to Arab Americans: Recommendations and considerations. *Cultural Diversity and Ethnic Minority Psychology, 7*(4), 308–327.

ESCWA and LAS. (2014). *Disability in the Arab region: An overview.* Retrieved from www.escwa.un.org/divisions/div_editor/Download.asp?table

Farah, L. G., Fayyad, J. A., Eapen, V., Cassir, Y., Salamoun, M. M., Tabet, C. C., . . . Karam, E. G. (2009). ADHD in the Arab world: A review of epidemiologic studies. *Journal of Attention Disorders, 13*(3), 211–222.

Ferrara, K., Burns, J., & Mills, H. (2015). Public attitudes toward people with intellectual disabilities after viewing Olympic or Paralympic performance. *Adapted Physical Activity Quarterly, 32*, 19–33.

Frisby, C. K., & Reynolds, C. R. (Eds.). (2005). *Comprehensive handbook of multicultural school psychology.* Hoboken, NJ: Wiley.

Gaad, E. (2010). *Inclusive education in the Middle East.* New York, NY: Routledge.

Gharaibeh, N. (2009). Disability in Arab societies. In K. Marshall, E. Kendall, M. Banks, & R. Gover (Eds.), *Disabilities: Insights from across fields and around the world* (pp. 63–80). Retrieved from xa.yimg.com/kq/groups/23895502/144661665/name/Disability

Global Deaf Muslim. (2010). *Qur'an into ASL.* Retrieved from http://globaldeafmuslim.org/index.php/programs/quran-into-asl

Goforth, A. N. (2011). Considerations for school psychologists working with Arab American children and families. *NASP Communique, 39*(6). Retrieved from www.nasponline.org/publications/cq/39/6/Multicultural-Affairs.aspx

Gonzales, N., & Stickney, R. (2012). *Fire victim loses life's work.* Retrieved from www.nbcsandiego.com/news/local/Professional-Photographer-House-Fire-San-Carlos-144621525.html

Habib, R. (2007). *Overview of the occupational safety and health situation in the Arab region.* Retrieved from www.oicvet.org/files/pilot-ALO_Study_En.doc

Haboush, K. L. (2007). Working with Arab American families: Culturally competent practice for school psychologists. *Psychology in the Schools, 44,* 183–198.

Hatton, C., Akram, Y., Robertson, J., Shah, R., & Emerson, E. (2003). The disclosure process and its impact on South Asian families with a child with severe intellectual disabilities. *Journal of Applied Research in Intellectual Disabilities, 16,* 177–188.

Higher Council for Persons with Disabilities. (2007). *Jordanian Law of Rights of Persons with Disabilities (Number 31).* Retrieved from www.hcd.gov.jo

Hijazi, S. (2014, February 21). Arab parents often hesitant in acknowledging children with autism. *The Arab American News.* Retrieved from www.arabamerican news.com/ news/ news/id_8312/Arab-parents-often-hesitant-in-acknowledging-children-with-autism.html

Hixson, L., Hepler, B. B., & Kim, M. O. (2011). The White population: 2010. *2010 Census Briefs* (C2010BR-05). Retrieved from www.census.gov/prod/cen2010/ briefs/c2010br-05.pdf

Hubert, J. (2006). Family carers' views of services for people with learning disabilities from Black and minority ethnic groups: A qualitative study of 30 families in a south London borough. *Disability & Society, 21,* 259–272.

Institute for Middle East Understanding. (2006). *Maysoon Zayid: Actor and comedian.* Retrieved from imeu.org/article/maysoon-zayid-actor-and-comedian

Jamil, H. (2002). A retrospective study of Arab American mental health clients: Trauma and the Iraqi refugees. *American Journal of Orthopsychiatry, 72*(3), 355–361.

Japan International Cooperation Agency. (2002). *Country profile on disability: Arab Republic of Egypt.* Retrieved from digitalcommons.ilr.cornell.edu

Kabbara, N. (2014, September 5). People with disabilities in the Arab world need more rights. *News and Media: United Nations Radio.* Retrieved from www. unmultimedia.org/radio/english/2014/09/people-with-disabilities-in-the-arab-world-need-more-rights/#.VMsAKGjF8xA

Kira, I. A., Lewandowski, L., Ashby, J. S., Templin, T., Ramaswamy, V., & Mohanesh, J. (2014). The traumatogenic dynamics of internalized stigma of mental illness among Arab American, Muslim, and refugee clients. *Journal of the American Psychiatric Nurses Association, 20*(4), 250–266.

Kronfol, N. M. (2012). Health services to groups with special needs in the Arab world: A review. *Eastern Mediterranean Health Journal, 18*(12), 1247–1253.

Kuaider, S. M. (2005). *Ecocultural study of Arab American families of children with disabilities* (Master's thesis). Long Beach, CA: California State University.

Lake, B. (2014). *Arab Americans are marginalized and overwhelmed with untrue stereotypes.* Retrieved from www.collegian.com/. . ./arab-americans. . .margi

Leubsdorf, B. (2009). Seeing-eye horse guides blind Muslim woman. *Health Care on NBC News.com.* Retrieved from www.nbcnews.com/id/30155540/ns/health-health_care/t/seeing-eye-horse-guides-blind-muslim-woman/#.VMusamjF8xA

MADA Qatar Assistive Technology Center. (2012). *An open call for the development of assistive technologies to support the needs of Arabic speaking disabled people.* Retrieved from http://mada.org.qa/en/wp-content/uploads/2012/02/call-for-assistive-technologies-to-support-disabled-people-in-Qatar.pdf

Manning, S. (2011). Miniature horses get OK to be service animals. *Today: Pets and Animals.* Retrieved from www.today.com/id/42378784/ns/today-today_pets/t/miniature-horses-get-ok-be-service-animals/#.VN-LQfnF8xA

McGrother, C. W., Bhaumik, S., Thorp, C. F., Watson, J. M., & Taub, N. A. (2002). Prevalence, morbidity and service need among South Asian and white adults with intellectual disability in Leicestershire, UK. *Journal of Intellectual Disability Research, 46,* 299–309.

Meyer, N., & Ibrahim, F. (2011, October 15). Suffering in silence: Arab Americans struggle to overcome mental health stigmas. *The Arab American News.* Retrieved from http://newamericamedia.org/2011/12/suffering-in-silence-arab-americans-struggle-to-overcome-mental-health-stigmas.php

Mokdad, A. H., Jaber, S., Abdel Aziz, M. I., AlBuhairan, F., AlGhaithi, A., AlHamad, N. M., . . .(2014). The state of health in the Arab world, 1990–2010: An analysis of the burden of diseases, injuries, and risk factors. *Lancet, 25,* 309–320.

Mont, D. (2007, March). *Measuring disability prevalence.* Retrieved from http://siteresources.worldbank.org/DISABILITY/Resources/Data/MontPrevalence.pdf

Moradi, B., & Hasan, N. T. (2004). Arab American persons' reported experiences of discrimination and mental health: The mediating role of personal control. *Journal of Counseling Psychology, 51*(4), 418–428.

Nagata, K. K. (2007). *The scale of attitudes towards disabled persons (SADP): Cross-cultural validation in a middle income Arab country, Jordan.* Retrieved from www.rds.hawaii.edu/ojs/index.php/journal/article/view/275/855

Nagata, K. K. (2008). Disability and development: Is the rights model of disability valid in the Arab region? *Asia Pacific Disability Rehabilitation Journal, 19*(1), 60–78.

National Disability Authority. (2010). *Literature review on attitudes towards disability.* Retrieved from www.ucd.ie/issda/static/documentation/nda/nda-literature-review.pdf

Office of the U. N. Special Rapporteur on Disability. (2007). *War, armed conflict, & disability challenges, statistics, facts.* Retrieved from www.srdisability.org/presentations/presentation_war_oct07.html

Oliver, B. (2014). Dearborn man helping others with visual impairments. *Times-Herald.* Retrieved from http://downriversundaytimes.com/2014/06/08/dearborn-man-helping-others-with-visual-impairments/

Olson, J. (2013). Autism hits Somali kids harder, University of Minnesota study finds. *Star Tribune Health.* Retrieved from www.startribune.com/lifestyle/health/236033201.html

Partain, R. (n.d.). Young Arab American is an inspiration and a strong voice for the disabled. *Arab America.* Retrieved from http://old.arabamerica.com/news.php?id=4905

Ravindran, N., & Myers, B. J. (2012). Cultural influences on perception of health, illness, and disability: A review and focus on autism. *Journal of Child and Family Studies, 21*(2), 311–319.

Read, J. G., Amick, B., & Donato, K. M. (2005). Arab immigrants: A new case for ethnicity and health? *Social Science and Medicine, 61*(1), 77–82.

Saif, I. (2013). *Arab economies in transition: Limited room for optimism.* Retrieved from http://carnegie-mec.org/publications/?fa=50415&lang=en

Scalenghe, S. (2014). *Disability in the Ottoman Arab World, 1500–1800.* New York, NY: Cambridge University Press.

Scior, K., Addai-Davies, J., Kenyon, M., & Sheridan, J. C. (2013). Stigma, public awareness about intellectual disability and attitudes to inclusion among different ethnic groups. *Journal of Intellectual Disability Research, 57*(11), 1014–1026.

Semlali, A. (2013). Obesity and traffic fatalities endemic to Arab world. *Aljazeera.* Retrieved from www.aljazeera.com/indepth/opinion/2013/07/2013721800293592.html

Tadmouri, G. O. (2013). *Genetic disorders in Arab populations.* Retrieved from www.cags.org.ae/cbc02ga.pdf

TED. (2014). *Maysoon Zayid: Comedian and writer.* Retrieved from www.ted.com/speakers/maysoon_zayid

Teebi, A. S., & Farag, T. I. (1997). *Genetic disorders among Arab populations.* New York, NY: Oxford University Press.

U.S. Census Bureau. (1997). *Disabilities affect one-fifth of all Americans.* Census brief. Retrieved from www.census.gov/prod/3/97pubs/cenbr975.pdf

U.S. Census Bureau. (2010). *American community survey 1-year estimates.* Retrieved from www.census.gov/acs/www

Westbrook, M., Legge, V., & Pennay, M. (1993). Attitudes towards disabilities in a multicultural society. *Social Science & Medicine, 36*(5), 615–623.

Wolcott, L. (2011). *A miniature guide horse in Lansing.* Retrieved from www.capitalgainsmedia.com/features/cali0511.aspx

World Bank. (2005). *A note on disability issues in the Middle East and North Africa.* Retrieved from www-wds.worldbank.org/external/default/WDSContentServer/WDSP/IB

World Bank. (2014). *Arab world.* Retrieved from http://data.worldbank.org/region/ARB

World Health Organization. (2011). *World report on disability.* Retrieved from whqlibdoc.who.int/publications/2011/ 9789240685215_eng.pdf

Yousef, J. M. (1993). Education of children with mental retardation in the Arab countries. *Mental Retardation, 31*(2), 117–121.

Further Readings

Arab American Family Service website. (n. d.). *Tutoring program tackles problems to ensure early intervention.* Retrieved from arabamericanfamilyservices.org

Balcazar, F. E., Garcia-Iriarte, E., Suarez-Balcazar, Y., & Taylor-Ritzler, T. (2008). Conducting disability research with people from diverse ethnic groups: Challenges and opportunities. *Journal of Rehabilitation, 74*(1), 4–11.

Cavenaugh, B. S., Giesen, J. M., & Sansing, W. K. (2001). Access to vocational rehabilitation: The impact of race and ethnicity. *Journal of Visual Impairment & Blindness, 98*(7), 410–419.

Czechowicz, S., Fujiura, G. T., & Yamaki, K. (1998). Disability among ethnic and racial minorities in the United States. *Journal of Disability Policy Studies, 9*(2), 111–130.

Dziekan, K. I., & Okocha, A. G. (1993). Accessibility of rehabilitation services: Comparison by racial-ethnic status. *Rehabilitation Counseling Bulletin, 36*(4), 183–189.

Hadidi, M. (1998). Educational programs for children with special needs in Jordan. *Journal of Intellectual and Developmental Disabilities, 23*(2), 147–154.

Hamdy, N. N., Auter, P. J., Humphrey, P. J., & Attia, A. (2011). A cultural perspective: A survey of U.S. and Egyptian students regarding their perceptions of people with disabilities. *International Journal of Humanities and Social Science, 1*(5), 83–93.

Hernandez, B. (2009). The disability and employment survey: Assessing employment concerns among people with disabilities and racial/ethnic minorities. *Journal of Applied Rehabilitation Counseling, 40*(1), 4–13.

Yosef, A. R. O. (2008). Health beliefs, practice, and priorities for health care of Arab Muslims in the United States. *Journal of Transcultural Nursing, 19*(3), 284–291.

3 Arab American Children with Disabilities and Special Education in the United States

The goals of this chapter are fourfold. The first goal is to provide an overview of the special education system in the United States. The second goal is to outline issues related to providing special educational services to racial and ethnic minority children with disabilities in the United States. The third goal is to discuss the time-consuming and complicated task of navigating this system. The fourth goal of this chapter is to discuss potential barriers to the use of special education programs and services by Arab American families.

Special Education in the United States: A Brief Overview

The Individuals with Disabilities Education Act (IDEA) of 1990, which was amended by Congress in 2004 and renamed the Individuals with Disabilities Education Improvement Act is the special education law in the United States. IDEA entitles all children with disabilities throughout the United States a free appropriate public education (FAPE) in the least restrictive environment (LRE). The disability categories listed in IDEA are as follows: autism, deaf–blindness, deafness, emotional disturbance, hearing impairment, intellectual disability, multiple disabilities, orthopedic impairment, other health impairment, specific learning disability, speech or language impairment, traumatic brain injury, or visual impairment (including blindness).

IDEA requires that students suspected of any of the categories of disabilities outlined previously should undergo an individual, comprehensive, multidisciplinary evaluation to determine their eligibility for special education. Such an evaluation must be

> (a) nondiscriminatory; (b) in the student's native language or other appropriate mode and in a manner that best measures the student's academic, developmental, and functional abilities; (c) valid and reliable; (d) administered by trained personnel according to the instructions

provided by the assessment's producer; (e) capable of assessing the student in all areas appropriate to the suspected disability including health, vision, hearing, social and emotional skills, general intelligence, academic performance, communication, and motor abilities; and (f) able to accurately measure the student's skills despite any sensory, manual, or speaking impairments. . . . Finally, any identified disability must not be the result of the student's limited English proficiency or receipt of inappropriate instruction in reading or math.

(Donovan, 2013, pp. 34–36)

IDEA also mandates that an individualized education program (IEP) be developed for each student receiving special education. The IEP is developed by a team that must include the professionals who work with the student and at least one parent. The IEP must include the following elements (Office of Special Education and Rehabilitation Services, U.S. Department of Education, 2000):

1   The student's current levels of performance
2   Annual goals broken down by short-term objectives
3   Special education and related services to be provided to the student
4   The extent, if any, to which the student will not participate with nondisabled students in the regular class
5   Modifications needed for the student's participation in state and districtwide tests
6   Projected date for the beginning of the services, as well as their frequency, location, and duration
7   Beginning at age 14, and updated annually, a statement of needed transition services
8   A statement of how the student's progress toward his or her annual goals will be measured

A major principle of IDEA is the Zero Reject principle, which ensures that no child with disabilities may be excluded from a public education, regardless of the nature or severity of the disability (Heward, 2012). Another provision of IDEA is parent and student participation. IDEA provides for shared decision making among schools, parents, and students with disabilities. Parents have the right to participate in decisions related to IEPs, related services, and placement decisions (Heward, 2012); furthermore, IDEA mandates that schools protect the rights of children with disabilities and their parents. In other words, due process safeguards that make schools and parents accountable to each other will be in place. Such safeguards include but are not limited to obtaining parental consent for evaluations and reevaluations, placement decisions, maintaining the confidentiality of the child records and making those records available to the parents, and obtaining an independent evaluation of the child when parents disagree with the results of a school evaluation (Heward, 2012).

IDEA includes procedural safeguards to protect the rights of parents and their children with disabilities. Arab American parents having children with disabilities, like all American parents, have the same rights. IDEA procedural safeguards can be found in Arabic on the Ohio Department of Education (2010) website. The Center for Parent Information and Resources (2014) and Advocates for Justice and Education (2010) list the following safeguards:

- Giving parents a complete explanation of all the procedural safeguards
- Providing parents "prior written notice" on matters relating to the assessment or placement of their child and the provision of special education and related services to their child
- Getting parental consent before their children are evaluated, provided services, or reevaluated
- Assuring parents of the confidentiality of their children's educational records and their right to inspect and review these records
- Facilitating parents' participation in meetings related to the identification, evaluation, and placement of their child, and the provision of FAPE (a free appropriate public education) to their child
- Ensuring parents' right to obtain an independent educational evaluation (IEE) of their child
- Ensuring parents' right to disagree with the school and to use mediation, due process hearings, or state complaints to resolve their disagreements

Special Education and Minority Ethnic Children with Disabilities

Notably, IDEA, first passed by Congress in 1975 as the Education of All Handicapped Children Act (Public Law 94–142), required that all children with disabilities must be provided equal access to education. American children with Arab roots who have disabilities, just like all other racial and ethnic minority children, are implicitly included. This segment of American society, regardless of its size or social standing, deserves adequate attention. Furthermore, the No Child Left Behind (NCLB) legislation, authorized in 2002 as Public Law 107–110, required raising the achievement levels of all students, regardless of race, income level, English language proficiency, or disability (Burke, 2012). Yet, disproportionality (overrepresentation or underrepresentation) of racial and ethnic minorities and English language learners (children whose native language is a language other than English) has been well documented over the past three decades (Drakeford, 2004; US Commission on Civil Rights, 2009). Contributing factors to disproportionality include economic disadvantage, student race, culture, language, assessment policies and practices, poverty, special education processes, inequity in general education, and issues of behavior management (National Education Association (2007; Skiba et al., 2008).

The literature shows disproportional prevalence rates of disability among racial and ethnic minority populations (Donovan, 2013; Houtenville, Sevak, O'Neill, & Cardoso, 2014; U.S. Census Bureau, 2000). Research reveals that the prevalence of disability among most racial and ethnic minority groups is higher than in the non-Hispanic White population (Advisory Committee on Minority Health, 2011; Benjamin, Wallace, Villa, & McCarthy, 2000). Disability prevalence among racial and ethnic groups in the United States varies, ranging from 20.5% among African Americans to 12.4% among Asian Americans (Yee, 2011). The literature also describes minorities with disabilities as encountering a "double burden" and "double discrimination" (Advisory Committee on Minority Health, 2011; Yee, 2011).

Other non-Arab Middle Eastern Americans (Iranian Americans, Turkish Americans) are also classified by the U.S. Census as "White" (Marvasti & McKinney, 2004). Like Arab Americans, Iranian Americans and Turkish Americans tend to hold on to elements of their cultures of origin (Hasnain, Shaikh, & Shanawani, 2008). These two minority groups have been at least as successful educationally and economically as Arab Americans in the United States. Because of their religion (Islam), color (brown skin), and unfamiliar names, these two minorities are generally subjected, like Arab Americans, to stereotypes and discrimination in the workplace, schools, medical settings, and several other public places (Marvasti & McKinney, 2004).

Like literature on Arab Americans with disabilities, literature pertaining to Turkish and Iranian Americans with disabilities is sparse. Disability-related published literature focuses almost exclusively on Iranians and Turkish persons with disabilities in their native lands. Like other Middle Eastern countries, Turkey (Firat, 2010) and Iran (Alaedini, 2004) utilize World Health Organization's (WHO) forecasts of disability prevalence rates because national statistical information on persons with disabilities is lacking. According to Moore and Kornblet (2011), stigma and lack of recognition of the needs of persons with disabilities are major impediments to progress in serving this population in both Iran and Turkey (Diken, 2006; Hasnain et al., 2008; Moore & Kornblet, 2011). Although both countries have recently emphasized educating students with disabilities in regular public schools, special education systems still focus on teaching and training students with disabilities in segregated educational settings in both Turkey (Melekoglu, Cakiroglu, & Malmgren, 2009) and Iran (Shokoohi-Yekta & Hendrickson, 2010). Other challenges faced in educating children with disabilities in Turkey and Iran include the scarcity of trained special education teachers and adequate schools, inadequate funding for special education programs, and limited research on special education (Melekoglu et al., 2009).

Benjamin et al. (2000) also asserted that determining the prevalence of disability among a population clarifies the limitations of people and their need for assistance in daily life. These authors also emphasized that identifying the prevalence of disability among immigrants is necessary for developing health and social service programs that meet their needs. Responding to the growing presence of diverse cultural groups in American society, the Council for Exceptional Children (CEC), America's premier association for special education professionals and the largest international professional organization dedicated to improving special education services, endorsed high-quality educational services to students with disabilities from diverse cultures (Council for Exceptional Children, 2008). Specifically, the CEC advocated (a) educational practices that appropriately identify students from diverse cultures who receive special education; (b) assessment practices that accurately reflect cultural differences; (c) education services that provide effective interventions for students from diverse cultures; (d) an increase in the number of diverse teachers, administrators, and university faculty from diverse cultures; and (e) professional development to improve the cultural competence of all educators.

The professional standards on multicultural knowledge and skills necessary for special education practitioners developed by the CEC (2009) included a total of 23 multicultural competencies, organized into the following eight domains: assessment, beliefs or historical perspectives, communication, English as second language, home and school, instruction, learning differences, and learning environments (see Table 3.1).

Similarly, the code of professional ethics for rehabilitation counselors adopted by the Commission on Rehabilitation Counselor Certification (2009) addressed issues related to multiculturalism and diversity. This code emphasized (a) respect for the cultural background of clients; (b) nondiscrimination based on age, color, race, culture, disability, ethnicity, gender, religion, language preference, socioeconomic status, or any basis proscribed by law; (c) beliefs, attitudes, knowledge, and skills regarding cultural meanings of confidentiality and privacy; (d) collaborative relationships with parents or guardians to best serve clients; (e) interventions and services to incorporate consideration of cultural perspective of clients; (f) caution with assessment techniques that were normed on populations other than that

Table 3.1 Multicultural Competencies for Special Education Practitioners

Assessment
- Administer nonbiased formal and informal assessments.
- Use assessment information in making eligibility, program, and placement decisions for individuals with exceptional learning needs, including those from culturally and/or linguistically diverse.

Beliefs/Historical Perspectives
- Issues in definition and identification of individuals with exceptional learning needs, including those from culturally and linguistically diverse backgrounds. Historical points of view and contribution of culturally diverse groups.
- Impact of the dominant culture on shaping schools and the individuals who study and work in them.
- Variations in beliefs, traditions, and values across and within cultures and their effects on relationships among individuals with exceptional learning needs, family, and schooling. Strategies used by diverse populations to cope with a legacy of former and continuing racism. Personal cultural biases and differences that affect one's teaching.

Communication
- Culturally responsive factors that promote effective communication and collaboration with individuals with exceptional learning needs, families, school personnel, and community members.
- Communicate effectively with families of individuals with exceptional learning needs from diverse backgrounds.
- Ways of behaving and communicating among cultures that can lead to misinterpretation and misunderstanding.
- Demonstrate sensitivity for the culture, language, religion, gender, disability, socioeconomic status, and sexual orientation of individuals.

English as Second Language
- Use communication strategies and resources to facilitate understanding of subject matter for students whose primary language is not the dominant language.

Home and School
- Cultural perspectives influencing the relationships among families, schools, and communities as related to instruction.
- Characteristics and effects of the cultural and environmental milieu of the individual with exceptional learning needs and the family. Potential impact of differences in values, languages, and customs that can exist between the home and school.

Instruction
- Strategies to prepare individuals to live harmoniously and productively in a culturally diverse world.
- Develop and select instructional content, resources, and strategies that respond to cultural, linguistic, and gender differences.
- Impact of learners' academic and social abilities, attitudes, interests, and values on instruction and career development.

- Prepare individuals to exhibit self-enhancing behavior in response to societal attitudes and actions.

Learning Differences
- Differing ways of learning of individuals with exceptional learning needs including those from culturally diverse backgrounds and strategies for addressing these differences.
- Teacher attitudes and behaviors that influence behavior of individuals with exceptional learning needs.
- Effects of cultural and linguistic differences on growth and development. Characteristics of one's own culture and use of language and the ways in which these can differ from other cultures and uses of languages.

Learning Environments
- Create a safe, equitable, positive, and supportive learning environment in which diversities are valued.
- Organize, develop, and sustain learning environments that support positive intracultural and intercultural experiences.
- Ways to create learning environments that allow individuals to retain and appreciate their own and each other's respective language and cultural heritage. Ways specific cultures are negatively stereotyped.
- Mediate controversial intercultural issues among students within the learning environment in ways that enhance any culture, group, or person.

Source: Council for Exceptional Children (2009).

of the client; (g) material related to cultural diversity into all courses and workshops for the development of professional rehabilitation counselors; (h) recruitment and retention of a diverse faculty and student body; and (i) cultural diversity competency into rehabilitation counseling training and supervision practices.

Helping Arab American Parents Navigate the Special Education System

Like all parents of children with disabilities, Arab American parents engage in the time- consuming and complicated task of navigating the American special education system to secure the services that meet their children's needs. One might expect that recent Arab immigrant families, especially those whose children have received special education in their native countries would face a challenging transition when they seek special education and related services for their children in the United States. These families' children are introduced to educational services unavailable in their native countries. The special education system in the United States is governed by national legislative guiding principles and procedures and works in a structured, systematic way. Guides to navigating the special education system in the United States are offered by many state departments of education, disability-specific national organizations, or parent advocacy groups, among others. These guides generally offer background information on special education in the United States, special education laws and regulations, the special education process, helpful sources and links, and definitions of frequently used terms (e.g., Klose, 2010; Massachusetts Department of Education, n.d.). The websites of the 10 states with the largest concentration of Arab Americans (California, Michigan, New York, Florida, Texas, New Jersey, Illinois, Ohio, Massachusetts, and Pennsylvania) offer an Arab version of many policies and procedures related to special education, specific information about the special education system in their state, individualized education program forms, and several special education forms, such as parent information brochures and parental consent forms.

Potential Barriers to the Use of Special Education Among Arab Americans

Discrimination has been cited as a major barrier preventing recognized racial and ethnic minorities in the United States (i.e., African Americans, American Indians and Alaska Natives, Hispanic and Latino Americans, Asian Americans and Pacific Islanders) from receiving social and educational services (Department of Health and Human Services, 1999; Hampton, 1999; Nazroo, 2003). For instance, a supplement issued by the Department of Health and Human Services (1999) showed no sufficient studies about the rates of mental disorders in many smaller racial and ethnic groups, Arab Americans implicitly included among these groups, making it difficult to reach firm conclusions on the overall prevalence in those populations. Furthermore, this supplement documented striking disparities affecting mental health care of racial and ethnic minorities compared with Whites. These included less access to mental health services, poorer quality of mental health care, and underrepresentation in mental health research.

Very limited research has investigated Arab American parents' attitudes toward seeking special education and related services. Donovan (2013) also reported that some Arab American fathers actively denied their children had disabilities. Other studies pertinent to help-seeking behavior among Arabs and Arab Americans were mostly related to mental health counseling and social work (e.g., Al-Busaidi, 2010; Al-Krenawi & Graham, 2000; Aloud, 2004; Amri & Bernak, 2012). The primary implication of these studies is that social stigma surrounding mental health problems and disability can be profound for Arab and Muslim Americans. As Amri and Bernak (2012) implied, minority and immigrant communities, including Arab and Muslim

Americans, may be reluctant to seek out mental health or special education services because they fear being stigmatized in their communities. In light of the findings of these studies, one can speculate that seeking special education among Arab Americans is most likely affected by cultural beliefs about disabilities, knowledge and familiarity with formal special education and related services, perceived social stigma, and help-seeking preferences.

Although family participation in the special education process is a right protected and regulated by legislation in the United States (Turnbull & Morningstar, 1993), no legislation exists concerning the involvement of parents in the special educational process in many other countries, including Arab countries. In Arab countries, special education practices have traditionally emphasized parent training and counseling and rarely involve the establishment of family–professional partnerships. Therefore, parent involvement and family–professional partnerships as perceived and practiced in the United States may be quite unfamiliar to many Arab American families, especially those who are recent immigrants.

With very few exceptions, families in Arab countries are generally viewed as needing counseling and guidance, but having very little to offer special education teachers; moreover, families are typically criticized and accused of being uncaring. For both teachers and researchers in Arab countries to point to lack of family understanding and cooperation as major obstacles hindering optimal outcomes is not uncommon. Although this might reflect teachers' and researchers' ignorance of parents' needs and potentials, the problem does not lie, however, completely in the attitudes of special education teachers and researchers. Many Arab families generally tend to accept as an established fact that the education of their children with disabilities is the sole responsibility of the school (Yousef & Hadidi, 1992).

Hence, a multitude of factors may impede Arab American parents' involvement in special education programs, especially recent Arab immigrants. First, most Arab American parents tend to view the school as the authority (Moosa, Karabenick, & Adams, 2001), a factor that may inhibit their participation. Donovan (2013) noted that parents may lack information about service delivery, parental rights, IEPs, and their children's disabilities. Some parents may be overwhelmed by the technical terminology used in special education and may be apprehensive about challenging school staff or requesting more special education services. In the Arab culture, parents tend to regard teachers as experts and will often defer educational decision making to them. As in many other cultures, parents' interference in their children's learning at the school may be considered disrespectful. For instance, Abadeh (2006) found that Arab American immigrant parents "were more comfortable following the teachers' suggestion without questioning" (p. 93). This possibly may be attributed to parents' previous experiences in Arab countries, where school personnel are viewed as authoritative and omnipotent (Abadeh, 2006; Donovan, 2013).

Another major factor that can be detrimental to Arab American parent involvement in their children's education is cultural beliefs. Moosa et al. (2001) found that very few mothers assisted in classrooms or other areas of the school. Teachers believed that "parent partnership with schools is not traditional in Arab culture" (p. 21); however, lack of Arab American parent involvement in education should not be misread as uncaring. Education is highly valued by Arab American parents, whose perception of involvement may simply differ from that of American parents.

In an attempt to avoid conflicts or disputes, some teachers opt for minimal communication with racial and ethnic minority parents, such as Arab Americans, because they are unfamiliar with these parents' cultural backgrounds and beliefs (Abadeh, 2006). Arab American parent involvement may also be hindered by language difficulties. In the study by Moosa et al. (2001), one teacher viewed Arab American parents' lack of involvement as reflecting language barriers. Donovan (2013) found that three Arab American mothers in her study needed help from parent advocates to understand their rights, communicate with teachers, understand special education laws, and participate meaningfully in their child's educational programs.

References

Abadeh, H. (2006). *Perceptions of Arab American parents with children with special needs regarding home–school communications* (Doctoral dissertation). Retrieved from ProQuest Dissertations and Theses database. (UMI No. 304972765).

Advisory Committee on Minority Health. (2011). *Assuring health equity for minority persons with disabilities: A statement of principles and recommendations.* Retrieved from www.qualitymall.org/products/prod2.asp?prodid=30219

Advocates for Justice and Education. (2010). *Parents' rights under IDEA.* Retrieved from www.directionservice.org/cadre/parent/artifacts/AJE-3%20Parents_Rights_Under_IDEA2010.pdf

Alaedini, P. (2004). *Training and employment of people with disabilities: Iran 2003.* Bangkok, Thailand: International Labor Office. Retrieved from digitalcommons. ilr.cornell.edu/cgi/viewcontent.cgi

Al-Busaidi, Z. Q. (2010). A qualitative study on the attitudes and beliefs towards help-seeking for emotional distress in Omani women and Omani general practitioners: Implications for post-graduate training. *Oman Medical Journal, 25,* 190–198.

Al-Krenawi, A., & Graham, J. R. (2000). Culturally sensitive social work practice with Arab clients in mental health settings. *Health & Social Work, 25*(1), 9–22.

Aloud, S. (2004). *Factors affecting attitudes toward seeking and using formal mental health and psychological services among Arab Muslim populations* (Doctoral dissertation). Retrieved from https://etd.ohiolink.edu/rws_etd/document/get/osu 1078935499/inline

Amri, S., & Bernak, F. (2012). Mental health help-seeking behaviors of Muslim immigrants in the United States: Overcoming social stigma and cultural mistrust. *Journal of Muslim Mental Health, 7*(1), 43–63.

Benjamin, A. E., Wallace, S. P., Villa, V., & McCarthy, K. (2000). *Disability and access to health and support services among California's immigrant populations.* Los Angeles, CA: UCLA Center for Health Policy Research. Retrieved from http://healthpolicy.ucla.edu/publications/ Documents/PDF/Disability%20 and%20Access%20to%20Health%20and%20Support.pdf

Burke, L. (2012). The student success act: Reforming federal accountability requirements under No Child Left Behind. *The Heritage Foundation.* Retrieved from www.heritage.org/research/reports/2012/01/student-success-act-reforming-no-child-left-behind

Center for Parent Information and Resources. (2014). *Parental rights under IDEA.* Retrieved from www.parentcenterhub.org/repository/parental-rights

Commission on Rehabilitation Counselor Certification. (2009). *Code of professional ethics for rehabilitation counselors.* Retrieved from www.oregon.gov/dhs/ vr/docs/crc-code-ethics.pdf

Council for Exceptional Children. (2008). *Council for Exceptional Children 2008 policy manual.* Retrieved from www.cec.sped.org

Council for Exceptional Children. (2009). *Professional standards on diversity.* Retrieved from www.cec.sped.org/About-Us/Diversity/Professional-Standards-on

Department of Health and Human Services. (1999). *Mental health: Culture, race and ethnicity.* Retrieved from www.ct.gov/dmhas/lib/dmhas/publications/mhethnicity.pdf

Diken, I. H. (2006). Turkish mothers' interpretation of the disability of their children with mental retardation. *International Journal of Special Education, 21*(2), 8–27.

Donovan, E. (2013). *A phenomenological exploration of Arab American parents' experiences with the special education process* (Doctoral dissertation). Retrieved from https://etd.ohiolink.edu/ap:0:0:APPLICATION_PROCESS=DOWNLOAD_ ETD_SUB_DOC_ACCNUM:::F1501_ID:kent1372583897,inline

Drakeford, W. (2004). *Racial disproportionality in school disciplinary practices.* Retrieved from www.nccrest.org/Briefs/School_Discipline_Brief.pdf

Firat, S. (2010). People with disabilities in Turkey: An overview. *Information Technologies, Management and Society, 3*(2), 51–54.

Hampton, N. Z. (1999). Meeting the unique needs of Asian Americans and Pacific Islanders with disabilities: A challenge to rehabilitation counselors in the 21st century. *Journal of Applied Rehabilitation Counseling.* Retrieved from www.ntac. hawaii.edu/ AAPIcourse/downloads/readings/pdf/MeetingtheNeeds.pdf

Hasnain, R., Shaikh, L.C., & Shanawani, H. (2008). *Disability and the Muslim perspective: An introduction for rehabilitation and health care providers.* Retrieved from http://cirrie.buffalo.edu/culture/monographs/muslim.pdf

Heward, W. L. (2012). *Exceptional children: An introduction to special education* (10th ed.). Upper Saddle River, NJ: Pearson/Prentice Hall.

Houtenville, A. J., Sevak, P., O'Neill, J., & Cardoso, E. (2014). Disability prevalence and economic outcomes. In D. Strauser (Ed.), *Career development, employment and disability in rehabilitation: From theory to practice* (pp. 11–40). New York, NY: Springer.

Klose, L. M. (2010). *Special education: A basic guide for parents.* Retrieved from www.nasponline.org/Documents/Resources and Publications/Handouts

Marvasti, A., & McKinney, K. D. (2004). *Middle Eastern lives in America.* Lanham, MD: Rowman & Littlefield.

Massachusetts Department of Education. (n.d.). *A parent's guide to special education.* Retrieved from www.fcsn.org/parents_guide/pgenglish.pdf

Melekoglu, M. A., Cakiroglu, O., & Malmgren, K. W. (2009). Special education in Turkey. *International Journal of Inclusive Education, 13*(3), 287–298.

Moore, A., & Kornblet, S. (2011). *Iran and America: A dialogue on disability.* Retrieved from iranprimer.usip.org/blog/2011/dec/03/iran-and-america

Moosa, S., Karabenick, S., & Adams, L. (2001). Teacher perceptions of Arab parent involvement in elementary schools. *School Community Journal, 11*(2), 7–26.

National Education Association. (2007). *Truth in labeling: Disproportionality in special education.* Retrieved from www.nccrest.org/Exemplars/Disporportionality_Truth_In_Labeling.pdf

Nazroo, J. Y. (2003). The structuring of ethnic inequalities in health: Economic position, racial discrimination, and racism. *American Journal of Public Health, 93*(2), 277–284.

Office of Special Education and Rehabilitation Services, U.S. Department of Education. (2000). *A guide to the individualized education program.* Washington, DC. Retrieved from www2.ed.gov/parents/needs/speced/iepguide/iepguide.pdf

Ohio Department of Education. (2010). *A parent's guide to the Individuals with Disabilities Education Improvement Act of 2004, IDEA* [in Arabic]. Retrieved from http://education.ohio.gov/getattachment/Topics/ Special-Education/Students-with-Disabilities/Physical-or-Mentally-Handicap/Whose-IDEA-Is-This-A-Parent-s-Guide-to-the-Individ/Whose-IDEA-Is-This-2010–11-Arabic.pdf.aspx

Shokoohi-Yekta, M., & Hendrickson, J. M. (2010). Friendships with peers with severe disabilities: American and Iranian secondary students' ideas about being a friend. *Education and Training in Autism and Developmental Disabilities, 45*(1), 23–37.

Skiba, R. J., Simmons, A. B., Ritter, S., Gibb, A. C., Rausch, M. K., & Cuadrado, J. (2008). Achieving equity in special education: History, status, and current challenges. *Exceptional Children, 74*(3), 264–288.

Turnbull, A. P., & Morningstar, M. E. (1993). Parent-professional interactions. In M. Snell (Ed.), *Systematic instruction of students with severe disabilities* (4th ed., pp. 31–60). Columbus, OH: Charles E. Merrill.

U.S. Census Bureau. (2000). *Disability status: 2000.* Retrieved from www.census.gov/prod/2003pubs/c2kbr-17.pdf

U.S. Commission on Civil Rights. (2009). *Minorities in special education.* Washington, DC. Retrieved from www.usccr.gov/pubs/MinoritiesinSpecialEducation.pdf

Yee, S. (2011). *Health and health care disparities among people with disabilities.* Retrieved from dredf.org/healthcare/Health-and-Health-Care-Disparities

Yousef, J. M., & Hadidi, M. (1992). Families of children with disabilities in Jordan. *International Journal of Disability, Development and Education, 39*(2), 127–133.

Further Readings

Coots, J. J. (2007). Building bridges with families: Honoring the mandates of IDEA. *Issues in Teacher Education, 16*(2), 33–40.

Leung, P. (1993). Minorities with disabilities and the Americans with Disabilities Act: A promise yet to be fulfilled. *Journal of Rehabilitation Administration, 17*(3), 92–100.

National Center for Learning Disabilities. (2006). *IDEA parent guide*. Retrieved from www.pacer.org/legislation/idea/pdf/idea2004parentguide.pdf

Ohio Department of Education. (2010). *Parent's guide to the Individuals with Disabilities Education Improvement Act (IDEA) of 2004*. Retrieved from education. ohio.gov/. . ./Whose-IDEA-Is-T

Olivos, E. M., Gallagher, R. J., & Aguilar, J. (2010). Fostering collaboration with culturally and linguistically diverse families of children with moderate to severe disabilities. *Journal of Educational & Psychological Consultation, 20*(1), 28–40.

4   Considerations in Working with Arab American Children with Disabilities

This chapter discusses special considerations for the delivery of culturally appropriate special education services for Arab American children with disabilities. These considerations include developing awareness of Arab culture, initiating outreach and awareness programs for Arab American families having children with disabilities, conducting appropriate assessment of Arab American children, promoting Arab American parent involvement in their children's education, assessing Arab American children's English language proficiency, addressing potential sources of overrepresentation of Arab American children in special education, and developing research-based information resources on Arab American children with disabilities. Obviously, teachers and service providers must use professional judgment in applying these considerations with each child and family individually.

As the number of Americans of Arab descent has grown significantly since the mid-1990s, so has the number of Arab American children with disabilities. This implies that special education and related service providers (e.g., school psychologists, school counselors, and social workers) are increasingly likely to work with an Arab American student with a disability. Arab Americans, however, remain the least studied ethnic group in the United States (*100 questions*, 2001; Derose, 2009; El-Badry, 1994; Moradi & Hasan, 2004; Vang, 2010), and literature on Arab American students in public schools is limited (Ferguson, 2004; Martin, 2009; Moosa, Karabenick, & Adams, 2001; Tabbah, 2011). Although the importance of addressing cultural and linguistic diversity is underscored in the delivery of special education and related services (Cartledge & Kourea, 2008; Gay, 2002; Kuykendall, 2012; Trent, Kea, & Oh, 2008) and research has been conducted on other racial minority groups (Artiles & Trent, 1994; Aud, Fox, & KewalRamani, 2010; Donovan & Cross, 2002; Hosp & Reschly, 2003; Johnson, Lessem, Bergquist, Carmichael, & Whitten, 2003; Losen & Orfield, 2002; Parrish, 2002; Skiba et al., 2008; Valles, 1998; Zhang & Katsiyannis, 2002), accurate information about Arab American children with disabilities and their families remains remarkably limited.

Considerations Related to Arab Culture and Family

The importance of developing culturally appropriate practices with Arab American children with disabilities and their families cannot be overstated. Arab Americans differ from the dominant culture as well as from other minority populations in terms of native languages, religious and social belief systems, and family structure. Aburumuh, Smith, and Ratcliffe (2009) found that teachers had limited understanding of Arab and Muslim children. Thus, teachers and service providers should increase their knowledge and appreciation of the Arab culture and develop an understanding of the social and political context within which the Arab American children and families are nested (Goforth, 2011).

Teachers and service providers also need to be aware of the differing communication styles of Arab American families. Most Arab Americans do not clearly state and emphasize what they want others to know. Instead, they tend to be less direct and depend highly on subtle messages that include use of body language, facial expression, and timing of silence (Al-Krenawi & Graham, 2000; Nobles & Sciarra, 2000). An awareness of these differing communication styles could contribute to more effective interaction with Arab American families and may prevent misunderstandings that might lead to conflict during the special education process (Kuaider, 2005). Hammoud, White, and Fetters (2005) noted that interactions with Arab Americans are facilitated by establishing personal relationships and understanding the nuances of communication, both verbal and nonverbal. When communicating with recent Arab American immigrants, service providers should assess language comprehension, and if needed, an interpreter should be used.

In the Arab culture, the individual's situation reflects on the entire family (Nobles & Sciarra, 2000); thus, the impact of disability on the family may be significant, and teachers and service providers should build trust with family members, not just with the child having a disability (Ezenkwele & Roodsari, 2013). Disability may have a profound impact particularly on mothers who in Arab culture, like in many other cultures, assume the ultimate responsibility of caring for their children with disabilities (Donovan, 2013). Because many Arab Americans generally are overinvolved with and overprotective of their family members, dependence in members with disabilities may be nurtured (Donovan, 2013). As in other cultures, Arab American parents experience a series of reactions upon diagnosis of a disability in their child (Donovan, 2013). These include shock, denial, disbelief, anger, guilt, grief, and stress. For Arab American parents, who are influenced by their culture, whose members view disability as something stigmatizing, learning that their child has a disability can be even more devastating than for parents in many other cultures (Diken, 2006; Reiter, Mar'i, & Rosenberg, 1986).

The family is the single most important social and economic institution for most Arabs. Arab society is built around the extended family system (Nydell, 1987). During stressful times (crisis, illness, or disability diagnosis), parents can rely on the whole family, including the extended family, to help them cope (Abudabbeh & Aseel, 1999). The extended family system may provide emotional support and financial assistance but may also limit the individual's independence. Members of Arab American extended families usually live near one another, spend a lot of time together, and are involved in one another's lives (Arab American National Museum, 2013). Arab immigrant families that transform from extended families to nuclear families commonly feel isolated and disengaged (Nobles & Sciarra, 2000). Another reason for their feelings of isolation and loneliness are the stark difference in the American lifestyle from the collectivist culture and community they had in their native country (Awad, 2010; Moradi & Hasan, 2004).

Considerations Related to Attitudes, Stigma, and Help-Seeking Among Arab Americans

Teachers and service providers will be better equipped to help Arab American persons with disabilities and their families if they attend to issues related to attitudes toward disability. Some researchers reported that attitudes toward persons with disabilities are more negative in collectivistic societies, like Arab societies, which emphasize group goals above individual needs and goals than in individualist societies that emphasize personal achievement (Nakamura as cited in Watanabe, 2006; Westbrook, Legge, & Pennay, 1993; Zaromatidis, Papadaki, & Glide, 1999). Literature published in the last decade confirmed that disability in Arab societies is more negatively perceived than in Western societies (Al Thani, 2006; Gharaibeh, 2009; Haboush, 2007; Nagata, 2007; Turmusani, 2003). Because of these negative attitudes, Arab Americans may seek counseling and other supportive services as a last resort (Donovan, 2013; Nobles & Sciarra, 2000). This might deprive their children with disabilities from the services they need, particularity early childhood intervention. Thus, intensive effort may be needed to convince Arab American families having at-risk children or children with disabilities to seek early intervention and counseling services.

The stress of raising a child with disability in Arab culture (Donovan, 2013; Haboush, 2007) may suggest an increased need for support and services to Arab American families having members with disabilities. Teachers and service providers need to think of methods to overcome obstacles they may encounter as a result of the stigma attached to disability in the Arab culture (Abudabbeh & Aseel, 1999; Al-Krenawi & Graham, 2000; Gharaibeh, 2009). Confidentiality of information regarding the person and his or her family also needs to be overemphasized because of the sense of shame related to disability (Donovan, 2013; Hakim-Larson, Kamoo, Nassar-McMillan, & Porcerelli, 2007).

Arab American families having a member with a disability need to know that the rights of individuals with disabilities in the United State are protected under both federal and state laws. Such laws include the Rehabilitation Act of 1973, the Education for All Handicapped Children Act of 1975, the Americans with Disabilities Act of 1990, the Individuals with Disabilities Education Act (IDEA) of 1997, and the No Child Left behind Act of 2001.

Cultural factors affect parents' help-seeking behaviors (Donovan, 2013; Lau & Takeuchi, 2001). Many Arab families tend to hide mental health problems and would seek treatment only as a last resort (Abudabbeh, 2005; Nassar-McMillan & Hakim-Larson, 2003; Nobles & Sciarra, 2000). Similarly, Arab and Muslim families tend to hide disability and are reluctant to seek disability-related services and personal support (Al-Krenawi & Graham, 2000; Hasnain, Shaikh, & Shanawani, 2008). Arab families do so because such a great stigma is attached to disability or because they commonly believe that disability must be endured because it is God's will. Arab Americans, like many other ethnic minorities, may be less likely to seek disability-related services because of factors such as language barriers, cultural and religious beliefs about special education and disabilities, gender role limitations, levels of acculturation, social class differences, differing perceptions of disability, lack of bilingual service providers and culture-fair assessment tools, and perceived discrimination and negative stereotyping (Boulos, 2011; Donovan, 2013; Hasnain et al., 2008).

As shown in Chapter 3, the Individuals with Disabilities Education Improvement Act (IDEA) of 2004 governs how states and public agencies provide special education and related services to U.S. children and guarantees the rights of all U.S. children with disabilities and their families regardless of race or religion. Accordingly, specific efforts should be made to assist minority children with disabilities and their parents assert their rights through legislation like IDEA (Balcazar, 2001). According to the National Council on Disability (2003)

> The best way to empower minorities with disabilities and their families to take full advantage of federal laws, programs, and services is to provide them with easy-to-understand, culturally appropriate information about what their rights are under various federal laws . . . and how best to exercise those rights when a violation occurs.
>
> (p. 10)

Given Arab Americans' possible lack of awareness of special education procedures and practices in the United States (Donovan, 2013), school personnel should clearly explain the special education process to them. Specifically, parents need to know the main principles of IDEA, such as free appropriate public education, individualized education program, least restrictive environment, parents' roles, and procedural safeguards.

Considerations Related to Assessment of Arab American Children

Assessment of Arab American children may pose special difficulties, especially for school psychologists who have little or no knowledge of the Arab American population. IDEA requires objective assessment practices when identifying children as having a disability. A main mandate of IDEA is nondiscriminatory assessment, meaning that tests must not be racially or culturally discriminatory; and they should be administered in the child's native or primary language. Furthermore, when a child is assessed, someone familiar with the child's cultural and linguistic background must be part of the assessment team (Burnette, 2000; Hardman, Drew, & Egan, 2010).

Information should be gathered about an Arab American child's English language proficiency during assessment (Goforth, 2011). Language may also play a role in the degree to which a child's assessment appears to reflect social–emotional difficulties (Haboush, 2007). Sayed (2003) noted that Arabic is a highly expressive language, which includes considerable repetition and emotion; therefore, Arab children may appear more disturbed than non-Arab children.

Teachers, counselors, and school psychologists should take into account Arab American culture and traditions when evaluating Arab American children (Goforth, 2011). They need to implement the assessment process in a culturally appropriate way. Given the significance of maintaining family honor and the stigma attached to disability and special education in the Arab culture, some Arab American parents refuse to refer their children to special education (Donovan, 2013; Haboush, 2007). These parents, especially fathers, struggle with accepting their children's placement in special education settings (Crabtree, 2007; Donovan, 2013). They believe that special education placements may result in lower self-esteem and self-expectations among children; thus, extensive work with Arab American families may be particularly important during initial stages of referral and assessment (Erickson & Al-Timimi, 2001; Goforth, 2011). Including the family in all decisions is important to help family members feel that their honor is maintained and to promote acceptability of the assessment process. Nassar-McMillan & Hakim-Larson (2003) also suggested using a multisystem, comprehensive approach when gathering information during the assessment process of Arab American children. For example, both immediate and extended family members can be invited to the meeting when conducting interviews. During the interviews, various kinds of information could be gathered, including levels of acculturation to the dominant culture, educational and childcare practices in their home country, and immigration history. Similarly, religion should be considered when evaluating Arab American children because religion is infused in Arab American ethnic and cultural identities, especially for Muslim Arab Americans (Goforth, 2011). Gender is also important to consider when providing services to Arab Americans, especially if the student is an adolescent (Goforth, 2011). Al-Krenawi and Graham (2000) suggested that maintaining certain gender boundaries is necessary. These include maintaining minimal eye contact, appropriate physical distance between the service provider and the student, and involving the family in the process.

Considerations Related to Arab American Parent Involvement in Their Children's Education

Parental active involvement in their children's education is strongly encouraged by IDEA. Disability-related laws in the United States emphasize developing collaborative partnerships between service providers and families of persons with disabilities (Turnbull & Turnbull, 2001). Extensive literature also provides strong evidence that family involvement has significant benefits in intervention programs (Bailey, Raspa, & Fox, 2012; deFur, 2012; Heward, 2012). Family involvement and support in these programs are at least as important for Arab American families with members with disabilities as for other families; however, service providers need to know that Arab family involvement in child's school (e.g., volunteering, observing, participating in special occasion activities, or attending IEP meetings) has been shown to be low to moderate (Abadeh, 2006; Donovan, 2013; Kuaider, 2005). Potential causes include language difficulties, viewing the school as the authority, parents' previous experiences with service providers in native countries, and time factors (Abadeh, 2006; Alkhateeb, Alhadidi, & Al Khatib, 2014; Alkhateeb, Alhadidi, & Alkhatib, 2015; Moosa et al., 2001; Taneije, 1998). Thus, family training and guidance are of critical importance when working with these families.

Many Arab Americans may find special education and related services in the United States complicated and confusing. According to Donovan (2013), these reactions could relate to their knowledge of special education practices based in the Arab world. The special education system in Arab countries, which is currently undeveloped, has no clear and actionable laws, lacks financial resources; and works differently from the special education system in the United States. In a paper on the delivery of health care to the Muslim Americans of Middle Eastern descent, Ezenkwele and Roodsari (2013) attributed this confusion to

> language barriers; cultural misconceptions; and perceptions of disrespect, discrimination, lack of knowledge about their religious and cultural practices, and gender preferences in seeking and accepting health care. . . . In addition, as a cultural norm arising from modesty and politeness, patients are frequently quiescent, more accepting of the health care hierarchy, and often try to remain unobtrusive. Patients do not verbalize their problem and may expect health care providers to anticipate their needs and situation.
>
> (p. 170)

In general, mothers are more involved than fathers in their children's education (Donovan, 2013; Kuaider, 2005). Arab American parents tend to be actively involved with their children's learning in the home environment (Kuaider, 2005; Moosa et al, 2001). Further, the Arab American cultural approach to an individual's autonomy and confidentiality may differ from the traditional American conception of these issues. Hammoud et al. (2005) explained culturally appropriate health services for Arab Americans:

> In providing care for patients from Arab and Muslim cultures, informed consent should be obtained in ways that are comprehensible and consistent with the person's language, customs, and culture. Unique to the United States is that the assessment of patients, care plans, and rules governing patient confidentiality are based on the concept of individual rights. In contrast, Arab and Muslim patients are likely to define themselves and their individual worth as relative to, rather than independent of, the rest of their family. Major decisions usually involve all members of the extended family, especially the men.
>
> (p. 1309)

Parent support groups can play an important role in providing parents with support and knowledge and in assisting them to manage the demands of having a child with a disability (Law, King, Stewart, & King, 2001); however, the few studies related to Arab American parent involvement with parent support and advocacy groups produced mixed results. Although Kuaider (2005) found that Arab American parents' involvement with disability networks and parent support groups was very low, Donovan (2013) found that some of the Arab American mothers she studied participated in informal advocacy experiences. Hence, service providers may need to explore factors inhibiting Arab

American parents' involvement with disability networks and parent support groups and develop strategies for enhancing their participation as appropriate.

Al-Hassan and Gardner (2002), the Family Empowerment and Disability Council (2012), and Thorp (1997) suggested a variety of strategies that can assist special educators in partnering with diverse families of children with disabilities. These strategies are most likely applicable to Arab American parents as well. First, logistical issues, such as flexibility in scheduling, childcare, and transportation, need to be addressed; furthermore, using teleconferencing and Web-based meetings and communications may help overcome logistical concerns of parents (Family Empowerment and Disability Council, 2012).

Second, parents with limited English language proficiency may feel neglected, discriminated against, or intimated and unable to effectively communicate their concerns. These parents may not understand the terminology and jargon related to their child's condition and needs or the special educational processes and policies (Al-Hassan & Gardner, 2002; Family Empowerment and Disability Council, 2012). Promising procedures in this regard include assessing and understanding the language needs of each family, including interpreters in meetings with parents, asking other parents who speak the same language to assist in the communication with the family, informing parents about their rights and responsibilities, and familiarizing them with the special educational practices in the United States (Al-Hassan & Gardner, 2002).

Third, parents of children with disabilities need timely, frequent, and precise information about their child's progress in a way that is understandable to them. The literature shows that this does not often happen (Family Empowerment and Disability Council, 2012; Thorp, 1997). Overcoming the barrier requires making school reports simple, using positive, direct, and simple language, using interpreters as necessary, attending to nonverbal communication, and developing a survival vocabulary list in the native language of the parent, and using technology to provide information to parents (Al-Hassan & Gardner, 2002; Family Empowerment and Disability Council, 2012; Thorp, 1997).

Fourth, teachers need to learn about their students' cultural background. Al-Hassan and Gardner (2002) and Thorp (1997) suggested that teachers read about other cultures, talk to families and understand their experiences, appreciate families' culture, welcome parents into the classroom, arrange for special cultural events in the school, and be careful with physical proximity and touching. The need, however, is obvious for avoiding overgeneralizations about families and their cultures. This important point has been succinctly explained by Thorp (1997):

> Formal diversity training implemented by some school systems most frequently focuses on describing specific cultures and cultural

practice. . . . Such information can lead to expectations for family participation that are based on stereotypes that may or may not hold true for any particular family. All families, in fact, vary greatly in the degree to which their beliefs and practices are representative of a particular culture, language group, religious group, or country of origin. Further, few cultures lend themselves to simple descriptors. . . . Current training approaches favor focusing on strategies for learning about each family's unique cultural experience and for using a cultural perspective to analyze interactions with families.

(p. 1)

Considerations Related to Arab American Children's English Language Proficiency

The children of recent Arab American immigrants possess varying levels of English fluency (Haboush, 2007). Language may represent a barrier to academic success for Arab American children whose native language is Arabic. Because some Arab American children have limited English language proficiency, several Arab American organizations (e.g., Arab American Action Network, Arab American Development Corporation, Arab-American Family Support Center, Brooklyn Arab American Friendship Center, Center for Arab American Philanthropy) developed programs to assist Arab Americans with English as a second language. Batalova and Margie (as cited in Khamis-Dakwar et al., 2012) reported evidence indicating that the number of Arabic-speaking English language learners (ELLs) in the United States has increased. In a study on Arab Americans in Detroit, Baker et al. (2004) found that 80% of their study sample reported they spoke English well or very well and that most were also bilingual. In another study, Suleiman (1999) found that 75% of all Arab Americans were able to speak English very well; however, some studies have reported significant numbers of Arab students with limited English proficiency (Martin, 2009). According to the 2000 U.S. Census (de la Cruz & Brittingham, 2003), 51% of Arab Americans spoke Arabic language at home; thus, an unknown number of Arab American students, like other language-minority students, may likely be misidentified as having special educational needs because of their trouble with English (Cummins, 2001).

According to the Connecticut Administrators of Programs for English Language Learners (CAPELL, 2011), when an English language learner (ELL), such as an Arab American child who is not proficient in English, experiences significant academic difficulties, determining whether the difficulties are the result of the language difference or a true disability that requires a referral to special education can be a challenge. The United States, which passed the No Child Left Behind Act in 2001, is currently addressing the challenge of effectively designing and implementing instruction for the growing population of bilingual ELLs, such as Arabic-speaking students. This is reflected in the increased interest in training of teachers of ELLs (e.g., Palmer, El-Ashry, Leclere, & Chang, 2007; Samson & Collins, 2012). When instructing ELLs, CAPELL (2011) cautioned against both overidentification (which may occur because several characteristics of typical ELLs may be mistaken as signs of learning or behavioral difficulties) and underidentification (because some school districts tend to wait a number of years before referring an ELL who may truly have a disability for special education and related services).

As the preceding paragraphs illustrate, many Arab American children need to acquire enough facility with the English language to meet the academic requirements of U.S. schools. Although the educational accommodations made by U.S. schools serve children from Arabic-speaking countries, issues and questions specific to them arise as schools strive to scaffold their transition into the English-speaking world of U.S. education (Palmer et al., 2007). The influence of the mother tongue may seriously affect Arabic-speaking learners' use of English. Alshayban (2012) observed that

> the Arabic language has features very different from English. These features include the use of definite articles, passive structure, sequence of the tense while using verbs, repetition of the subject, . . . and the writing system, since writing in English reads from left to write while writing in Arabic reads from right to left.
>
> (p. 7)

Children who are learning English as a second language, ELLs, are often significantly behind in academic achievement (Batchley & Lau, 2010). These children also often develop social and emotional problems when learning to live in a new culture and using a new language (CAPELL, 2011). Accordingly, they are at risk for referral for special education (Batchley & Lau, 2010). Minority children are typically disproportionately represented in special education in the United States (U.S. Commission on Civil Rights, 2009; Warger & Burnette, 2000; Zhang & Katsiyannis, 2002); therefore, some Arab American children, like other racial and ethnic minority children, are likely to be incorrectly identified as having a disability and consequently overrepresented in special education programs. IDEA requires that any identified disability must not be the result of the student's limited English proficiency (Donovan, 2013). In order to reduce the likelihood of a premature decision to refer children to special education, the Individuals with Disabilities Improvement Act of 2004 (IDEA, 2004) offered greater flexibility to schools by permitting the use of the Response to Intervention (RtI) approach as part of the evaluation process. RtI is a three-tiered approach to providing effective instruction to struggling children at increasing levels of intensity. Children are referred to special education evaluation only if they do not respond to the instruction (National Joint Committee on Learning Disabilities, 2005).

To avoid or reduce misdiagnosis or overrepresentation of minority or ELLs, IDEA (as cited in CAPELL, 2011) requires that

> the assessments and other evaluation materials used to assess a child must be selected and administered so as not to be discriminatory on racial or cultural basis. . . . They must be administered in a professional manner by competent personnel and must use the language and form most likely to yield accurate information on what the child knows and can do academically, developmentally, and functionally, unless it is not feasible to so provide or administer.

(p. 32)

Following is a summary of guidelines offered by Batchley and Lau (2010) for assessing ELLs:

1   Exercising considerable caution when sing nationally standardized, norm-referenced test (NRT) scores to determine eligibility of ELLs for special education.
2   Personnel involved in assessment and planning for ELLs should know how to work with interpreters.
3   Native and English communication assessments should be conducted. These assessments may (a) rule in or out a potential language disorder in the native language, (b) provide evidence of the strength of native language skills, (c) explore the potential relevance of bilingual instruction, and (d) aid interpretation of data from other areas of assessment. Collecting information about native language proficiency may be helpful in determining disabilities and instructional needs.
4   When assessing cognitive performance of ELLs, both language and cultural knowledge influence test performance; therefore, the student's degree of acculturation should be considered. Using nonverbal measures, despite having some limitations, may yield less discriminatory results for ELLs.
5   When assessing academic performance of ELLs, it is helpful to understand the current and previous instructional programs offered for the student.
6   When ELLs exhibit emotional or behavior problems, their stage of acculturation must be considered. Parent interviews and systematic observation of the student help reduce bias in the assessment of social–emotional and behavioral development.

Religion-Related Considerations

Consideration must be given to the role of religion in the life of Arab families because religion serves as an important context in which problems are constructed and resolved (Al-Krenawi & Graham, 2000). Although the majority of Arab Americans are Christian, the percentage of Arab Americans who are Muslim has increased (Arab American Institute, 2012). Published literature typically emphasizes giving consideration to the role of religion in moderating the impact of mental health problems or disability on Arab American individuals and families, whether Islamic or Christian (Al-Krenawi & Graham, 2000; Al Thani, 2006; Boulos, 2011; Crabtree, 2007; Erickson & Al-Timimi, 2001; Nobles & Sciarra, 2000).

Read (2003) examined the impact of religion on a national sample of Arab American women's gender role attitudes. Results revealed that women's roles were more a cultural trait among Arabs than an effect of Christian or Muslim religions. Hamdy (n. d.) also asserted that religion may not be a good predictor of family values among Arab Americans. According to this author, "Arab families are tightly knit well beyond the nuclear family itself. Christian and Muslim Arabs alike may keep a family-oriented way of conducting their lives while adapting to their immigrant environment in the US" (p. 4). Hence, a few statements about persons with disabilities from an Islamic perspective are relevant.

According to Islam, individuals are entitled to various rights, among them the rights to life, identity, family cohesion, personal freedoms, and sound upbringing. Other rights include education, appropriate social living standards, protection from all forms of abuse, and physical and psychological care (Organization of the Islamic Countries, 2004). Covenant on the rights of the child in Islam adopted by this organization includes one article about children with disabilities that emphasizes the right of the child with a disability to appropriate education, multidisciplinary care, and integration into society. Islam does not say a great deal about disability per se (Al Thani, 2006; Miles, 2007). Even the statements found in the Qur'an about disability—such as blindness and deafness—are ambiguous, often best understood figuratively or metaphorically (Al Thani, 2006; Miles, 2007); however, in Islam, disability is accepted as a fact of life that must be addressed appropriately by society (Almusa & Ferell, 2004). Positive social attitudes toward persons with disabilities or illnesses are clearly encouraged. One of the fundamental propositions of Islam is to respect and support all human life and to value the potential of every individual, and this fact does not change when a person has a disability (Almusa & Ferell, 2004; Guvercin, 2008). Furthermore, Islam calls for accepting all people and encourages including them. Prejudice against and exclusion of any group of people is opposed.

Considerations Related to Stereotypes and Acculturation

As mentioned earlier in this book, Arab Americans are frequently subjected to damaging stereotypes. Arab American individuals and their families want to feel respected, and providing special educators and other service providers with information about their culture and religion promotes understanding (Aburumuh et al., 2009; Schwartz, 1999). Furthermore, they may feel alienated because of perceived stereotyping, prejudice, and ridicule of their cultural rituals (Jackson, 1997). Discrimination can lead to a number of psychosocial problems, including depression, psychological distress, and low self-esteem (Al-Hazza & Bucher, 2010; Nobles & Sciarra, 2000). Thus, teachers and service providers must ensure that Arab American persons with disabilities are treated equitably and without prejudice (Al-Hazza & Bucher, 2010). In order to understand and help students, teachers and service providers must overcome their own prejudices, misconceptions, and knowledge gaps.

Nonetheless, acculturation experiences of Arab Americans are influenced by many other social and psychological factors, including religion, gender, language skills, education, time of immigration, reasons for immigration, economic status, and presence or absence of family support (Barry, 2005; Boulos, 2011; Ferguson, 2004; Nobles & Sciarra, 2000). In addition, differences in acculturation among persons from the three immigration waves are noticeable, with immigrants from the first wave more completely assimilated into American mainstream culture (Derose, 2009). According to Nobles and Sciarra (2000), well-acculturated Arab Americans tend to "have distant ancestral ties, be successful, have high leadership positions, advocate secularism, or identify with Christianity" (p. 185). Like many other ethnic and linguistic minority groups that experience acculturative stress, many Arab Americans encounter difficulties in assimilating into the dominant American culture (Arab American National Museum, 2013). They face difficulties as they strive to maintain their cultural heritage in which they take pride, while trying to become integrated into the American culture that promotes individualistic values. In general, assimilation into American culture is more difficult for Muslim Arab Americans than for Christian Arab Americans because of their different religious values (Ajrouch & Jamal, 2007; Jackson & Nassar-McMillan, 2006; Nassar-McMillan & Hakim-Larson, 2003).

Teachers and service providers must assess the level of acculturation of Arab American clients and modify their style and intervention accordingly (Dwairy, 2006). Several studies have indicated an association between acculturation and health and disease among Arab Americans (El-Sayed & Galea, 2009; El-Sayed, Tracy, Scarborough, & Galea, 2011; Hatahet, Khosla, & Fungwe, 2002; Jaber et al., 2003). One can infer from a study conducted by Sayed (2003) on psychotherapy of Arab patients in the West that providing counseling services to Arab American individuals with disabilities and their families who are not acculturated to the American way of life presents challenges to teachers and service providers. This is expected because of the contrasting cultural understanding and perceptions of disability and the service provision process; however, the researchers were unable to identify similar studies on acculturation issues and disability. Thus, research exploring the relationship between acculturation and disability management in this population is warranted.

To recap, special educators and service providers are working with increasing numbers of culturally and racially diverse populations. The importance of culturally appropriate approaches with racially and linguistically diverse persons with disabilities and their families has been emphasized in recent years (Irvine & Fenwick, 2009; Lichtenstein, Lindstrom, & Povenmire-Kirk, 2008; National Center on Secondary Education and Transition, 2004; Villegas & Irvine, 2010). Consistent with this approach, this chapter provided an overview of the following relevant cultural considerations when providing special education and related services to Arab Americans with disabilities and their families.

Considerations Related to Advocacy for Arab Americans with Disabilities

In the United States, parental advocacy efforts were a main factor in bringing about special educational reform for children with disabilities (Kritzer, 2012). However, as Haboush (2007) emphasized, advocacy for children around educational issues is largely unfamiliar to recently immigrated Arab American parents because disagreement with authority figures in most Arab countries is unfamiliar. Further, these parents may face barriers to advocating for their children with disabilities because of lack of knowledge of educational options and services available to children with disabilities, unfamiliarity with diagnostic criteria for disabilities in the United States, and lack of knowledge of procedural requirements of the IDEA (Phillips, 2008). Accordingly, efforts are needed to encourage Arab American parent advocacy groups and implement parent education and awareness training.

Like families of majority and minority background in the United States, Arab American families can benefit from advocacy efforts in understanding the rights of their children with disabilities. Such efforts also can help families educate others about their children's strengths and difficulties and encourage other Arab American parents to feel unapologetic about their own children's disabilities and to seek out special education services (Donovan, 2013). One such effort was recently carried out by two Arab American mothers of children with autism (Mona Alaoue and Mariam Alaoue) who established an autism awareness organization in Michigan called Blue Hands United of Dearborn. Special education advocacy efforts can also be mounted by organizations that are dedicated to raising awareness of the Arab American culture and representing the concerns of Arab Americans at the local and national levels. These organizations include the Arab Community Center for Economic and Social Services (ACCESS), Arab American Family Services (AAFS), American-Arab Anti-discrimination Committee (ADC), Arab American Institute (AAI), Arab American Association of New York (AAANY), National Arab American Medical Association (NAAMA), Arab American National Museum (AANA), and Network of Arab-American Professionals (NAAP).

Additionally, advocacy efforts can further be conducted by special education organizations, educators, and parents. IDEA 2004 authorized the establishment of Parent Training and Information (PTI) centers. These PTIs are found in every state in the United States and are parent-directed, nonprofit organizations. They offer parent-to-parent support, assistance for educational issues, information and referral, and resource library and information packets. Parent advocate volunteers attend IEP meetings, case reviews, juvenile court hearings, and treatment team meetings and encourage parents to advocate for their children and their family's needs. Table 4.1 shows the websites of PTIs in the 10 states in which Arab American populations are concentrated.

Table 4.1 Websites of PTIs in the States in Which Arab American Communities Are Concentrated

State	PTI Websites
California	www.taskca.org, www.epuchildren.org, http://dredf.org, www.matrixparents.org, www.php.com, www.supportfor families.org, www.warmlinefrc.org
Florida	http://fndusa.org, http://fndusa.org/contact-us/programs/pen, http://fndusa.org/contact-us/programs/popin
Illinois	www.frcd.org, www.fmptic.org
Massachusetts	http://fcsn.org
Michigan	www.michiganallianceforfamilies.org
New Jersey	www.spannj.org
New York	www.starbridgeinc.org, www.advocatesforchildren.org, www.includenyc.org, www.sinergiany.org, www.theliac.org, www.theliac.org
Ohio	www.ocecd.org
Pennsylvania	www.pealcenter.org
Texas	www.partnerstx.org/team, www.partnerstx.org/path, www.partnerstx.org/pen

References

100 questions and answers about Arab Americans. (2001). Retrieved from www. bintjbeil.com/E/news/100q/home.html

Abadeh, H. (2006). *Perceptions of Arab American parents with children with special needs regarding home–school communications* (Doctoral dissertation). Retrieved from ProQuest Dissertations and Theses database. (UMI No. 304972765).

Abudabbeh, N. (2005). Arab families: An overview. In M. McGoldrick, J. Giordano, & N. Garcia-Preto (Eds.), *Ethnicity and family therapy* (3rd ed., pp. 423–436). New York, NY: Guilford Press.

Abudabbeh, N., & Aseel, H. A. (1999). Transcultural counseling and Arab Americans. In J. McFadden (Ed.), *Transcultural counseling* (2nd ed., pp. 283–296). Alexandria, VA: American Counseling Association.

Aburumuh, H. A., Smith, H. L., & Ratcliffe, L. G. (2009). *Educators' cultural awareness and perceptions of Arab-American students: Breaking the cycle of ignorance.* Retrieved from libra.msra.cn/. . ./running-head-educators-awareness-and-perceptions-of-ara

Ajrouch, K. J., & Jamal, A. (2007). Assimilating to a white identity: The case of Arab Americans. *International Migration Review, 41*(4), 860–879.

Al-Hassan, S., & Gardner, R. III. (2002). Involving immigrant parents of students with disabilities in the educational process. *Teaching Exceptional Children, 34*(5), 52–58.

Al-Hazza, T. C., & Bucher, K. T. (2010). Bridging a cultural divide with literature about Arabs and Arab Americans. *Middle School Journal, 41*(3), 4–11.

Alkhateeb, J. M., Alhadidi, M. S., & Alkhatib, A. J. (2014). Arab Americans with disabilities and their families: A culturally appropriate approach for counselors. *Journal of Multicultural Counseling and Development, 42*, 232–247.

Alkhateeb, J. M., Alhadidi, M. S., & Alkhatib, A. J. (2015). Addressing the unique needs of Arab American children with disabilities. *Journal of Child and Family Studies, 24*(8), 2432–2440.

Al-Krenawi, A., & Graham, J. R. (2000). Culturally sensitive social work practice with Arab clients in mental health settings. *Health & Social Work, 25*(1), 9–22.

Almusa, A., & Ferell, K. (2004). *Blindness in Islam.* Retrieved from faculty.ksu.edu. sa/10607/DocLib5/Blindness%20in%20Islam.doc

Alshayban, A. S. (2012). *Copula omission by EFL Arab learners* (Master's thesis). Retrieved from http://digitool.library.colostate.edu/exlibris/dtl/d3_1/apache_media/L2V4bGlcmlzL2R0bC9kM18xL2FwYWNoZV9tZWRpYS8xNjE5MjI=.pdf

Al Thani, H. (2006). Disability in the Arab region: Current situation and prospects. *Journal for Disability and International Development, 3*, 4–9. Retrieved from www.iiz-dvv.de/index.php?article_id=137&clang=1

Arab American Institute. (2012). *Demographics.* Retrieved from www.aaiusa.org/pages/demographics

Arab American National Museum. (2012). *Arab Americans: An integral part of American society.* Retrieved from www.arabamericanmuseum.org/umages/pdfs/resource_booklets/ AANM-ArabAmericansBooklet-web.pdf

Arab American National Museum. (2013). *Arab American culture.* Retrieved from www.arabamericanmuseum.org/Arab+American+Culture.id.168.htm

Artiles, A. J., & Trent, S. C. (1994). Overrepresentation of minority students in special education: A continuing debate. *The Journal of Special Education, 27*(4), 410–438.

Aud, S., Fox, M. A., & KewalRamani, A. (2010). Status and trends in the education of racial and ethnic groups. *U.S. Department of Education.* Retrieved from nces.ed.gov/pubs2010/2010015.pdf

Awad, G. H. (2010). The impact of acculturation and religious identification on perceived discrimination for Arab/Middle Eastern Americans. *Cultural Diversity and Ethnic Minority Psychology, 16*(1), 59–67.

Bailey, D. B., Raspa, M., & Fox, L. C. (2012). What is the future of family outcomes and family-centered services? *Topics in Early Childhood Special Education, 31*(4), 216–223.

Baker, W., Howell, S., Jamal, A., Lin, A. C., Shryock, A., Stockton, R., & Tessler, M. (2004). *Preliminary findings from the Detroit Arab American study.* Retrieved from www.umich.edu/news/Releases/2004/Jul04/daas.pdf

Balcazar, F. E. (2001). Strategies for reaching out to minority individuals with disabilities. *Research Exchange, 6*(2), 9–13.

Barry, D. T. (2005). Measuring acculturation among male Arab immigrants in the United States: An exploratory study. *Journal of Immigrant Health, 7*(3), 179–184.

Batchley, L. A., & Lau, M. Y. (2010). *Culturally competent assessment of English language learners for special education services.* Retrieved from citeseerx.ist.psu.edu/viewdoc/download?doi=10.1.1.183.3195

Boulos, S. A. (2011). *The role of acculturation, ethnic identity, and religious fatalism on attitudes towards seeking psychological help among Coptic Americans* (Doctoral dissertation). Retrieved from http://repository.tamu.edu/bitstream/handle/1969.1/ETD-TAMU-2011-05-9426/BOULOS-DISSERTATION.pdf?sequence=2

Burnette, J. (2000). Assessment of culturally and linguistically diverse students for special education eligibility. *ERIC Clearinghouse on Disabilities and Gifted Education* (ERIC EC Digest #E604). Retrieved from www.hoagiesgifted.org/eric/e604.html

CAPELL. (2011). *English language learners and special education: A resource handbook.* Retrieved from www.sde.ct.gov/sde/lib/sde/pdf/curriculum/bilingual/CAPELL_SPED_resource_guide.pdf

Cartledge, G., & Kourea, L. (2008). Culturally responsive classrooms for culturally diverse students with and at risk for disabilities. *Exceptional Children, 74*(3), 351–371.

Crabtree, S. A. (2007). Culture, gender, and the influence of social change amongst Emirati families in the United Arab Emirates. *Journal of Comparative Family Studies, 38*, 575–587.

Cumming, J. (2001). Empowering minority students: A framework for intervention. *Harvard Educational Review, 71*(4), 649–675. Retrieved from www.reading.ccsu.edu/abadiano/courses/rdg503/rubrics/cummins.pdf

deFur, S. (2012). Parents as collaborators: Building partnerships with school-and community-based providers. *Teaching Exceptional Children, 44*(3), 58–67.

de la Cruz, G. P., & Brittingham, A. (2003). *The Arab population: 2000.* Washington, DC: U.S. Census Bureau. Retrieved from www.census.gov/prod/2003pubs/c2kbr-23.pdf

Derose, M. E. (2009). *Factors affecting Arab Americans' psychological health: Culture, religion, acculturation, and experiences of discrimination* (Doctoral dissertation). Retrieved from http://udini.proquest.com/view/factors-affecting-arab-americans-pqid:1949111201/

Diken, I. H. (2006). An overview of parental perceptions in cross-cultural groups on disability. *Childhood Education, 82*(4), 236–240.

Donovan, E. (2013). *A phenomenological exploration of Arab American parents' experiences with the special education process* (Doctoral dissertation). Retrieved from https://etd.ohiolink.edu/ap:0:0:APPLICATION_PROCESS=DOWNLOAD_ETD_SUB_DOC_ACCNUM:::F1501_ID:kent1372583897,inline

Donovan, M. S., & Cross, C. T. (Eds.). (2002). *Minority students in special and gifted education.* Washington, DC: National Academy Press.

Dwairy, M. (2006). *Counseling and psychotherapy with Arabs and Muslims: A culturally sensitive approach.* New York, NY: Teachers College Press.

El-Badry, S. (1994). The Arab-Americans. *American Demographics, 75*(1), 22–30.

El-Sayed, A. M., & Galea, S. (2009). The health of Arab-Americans living in the United States: A systematic review of the literature. *BMC Public Health, 9,* 272–280.

El-Sayed, A. M., Tracy, M., Scarborough, P., & Galea, S. (2011). Ethnic inequalities in mortality: The case of Arab Americans. *PLOS One, 6*(12). Retrieved from www.ncbi.nlm.nih.gov

Erickson, C. D., & Al-Timimi, N. R. (2001). Providing mental health services to Arab Americans: Recommendations and considerations. *Cultural Diversity and Ethnic Minority Psychology, 7*(4), 308–327.

Ezenkwele, U. A., & Roodsari, G. S. (2013). Cultural competencies in emergency medicine: Caring for Muslim-American patients from the Middle East. *Journal of Emergency Medicine, 45*(2), 168–174.

Family Empowerment and Disability Council. (2012). *The Individuals with Disabilities Education Act and parent participation.* Retrieved from www.efrconline.org/myadmin/files/fedc_Parent_Participation.pdf

Ferguson, C. J. (2004). Arab Americans: Acculturation and prejudice in an era of international conflicts. In C. Negy (Ed.), *Cross-cultural psychotherapy: Toward a critical understanding of diverse clients* (pp. 265–278). Reno, NV: Bent Tree Press.

Gharaibeh, N. (2009). Disability in Arab societies. In K. Marshall, E. Kendall, M. Banks, & R. Gover (Eds.), *Disabilities: Insights from across fields and around the world* (pp. 63–80). Retrieved from xa.yimg.com/kq/groups/23895502/144661665/name/Disability

Goforth, A. N. (2011). Considerations for school psychologists working with Arab American children and families. *NASP Communique, 39*(6). Retrieved from www.nasponline.org/publications/cq/39/6/Multicultural-Affairs.aspx

Guvercin, H. (2008). People with disabilities from an Islamic perspective. *The Fountain.* Retrieved from www.fountainmagazine.com/Issue/detail/People-with-Disabilities-from-an-Islamic-Perspective

Haboush, K. L. (2007). Working with Arab American families: Culturally competent practice for school psychologists. *Psychology in the Schools, 44,* 183–198.

Hakim-Larson, J., Kamoo, R., Nassar-McMillan, S. C., & Porcerelli, J. H. (2007). Counseling Arab and Chaldean American families. *Journal of Mental Health Counseling, 29*(4), 301–321.

Hamdy, K. (n.d.). *Arab and Muslim Americans: An introduction for educators.* Retrieved from www.cengage.com/resource_uploads/downloads/0495915297_257292.pdf

Hammoud, M. M., White, C. B., & Fetters, M. D. (2005). Opening cultural doors: Providing culturally sensitive healthcare to Arab American and American Muslim patients. *American Journal of Obstetrics and Gynecology, 193,* 1307–1311.

Hardman, M. L., Drew, C. J., & Egan, M. W. (2010). *Human exceptionality: School, community, and family* (10th ed.). Boston, MA: Cengage Learning.

Hasnain, R., Shaikh, L.C., & Shanawani, H. (2008). *Disability and the Muslim perspective: An introduction for rehabilitation and health care providers.* Retrieved from http://cirrie.buffalo.edu/culture/monographs/muslim.pdf

Hatahet, W., Khosla, P., & Fungwe, T. V. (2002). Prevalence of risk factors to coronary heart disease in an Arab-American population in southeast Michigan. *International Journal of Food Sciences Nutrition, 53*(4), 325–335.

Heward, W. L. (2012). *Exceptional children: An introduction to special education* (10th ed.). Upper Saddle River, NJ: Pearson/Prentice Hall.

Hosp, J. L., & Reschly, D. J. (2003). Referral rates for intervention or assessment: A meta-analysis of racial differences. *The Journal of Special Education, 37*(2), 67–80.

Irvine, J. J., & Fenwick, L. T. (2009). *Teachers and teaching for the new millennium: The role of HBCUs.* U.S. Department of Education. Retrieved from www.sanders.senate.gov/imo/media/doc/TeacherandTeachingfortheNewMillennium.TheRoleofHBCUs.pdf

Jaber, L. A., et al. (2003). Epidemiology of diabetes among Arab Americans. *Diabetes Care, 26*(2), 308–313.

Jackson, M. L. (1997). Counseling Arab Americans. In C. C. Lee (Ed.), *Multicultural issues in counseling* (2nd ed., pp. 333–352). Alexandria, VA: American Counseling Association.

Jackson, M. L., & Nassar-McMillan, S. C. (2006). Counseling Arab Americans. In C. C. Lee (Ed.), *Counseling for diversity* (3rd ed., pp. 135–147). Alexandria, VA: American Counseling Association.

Johnson, C., Lessem, A., Bergquist, C., Carmichael, D., & Whitten, G. (2003). *Disproportionate representation of minority children in special education.* Retrieved from www.emstac.org/registered/topics/disproportionality/intro.htm

Khamis-Dakwar, R., Al-Askary, H., Benmamoun, A., Ouali, H., Green, H., Leung, T., & Al-Asbahi, K. (2012). *Cultural and linguistic guidelines for language evaluation of Arab-American children using the Clinical Evaluation of Language*

Fundamentals (CELF). Retrieved from http://home.adelphi.edu/~nslplab/PDFS/BilingualServicestoASHA_WholeResource.pdf

Kritzer, J. B. (2012). Comparing special education in the United States and China. *International Journal of Special Education, 27*(2), 52–56.

Kuaider, S. M. (2005). *Ecocultural study of Arab American families of children with disabilities* (Master's thesis). Long Beach, CA: California State University.

Kuykendall, M. (2012). Strategies for cultural awareness of teachers in training: An action research project. *Delta Journal of Education, 2*(1), 27–41.

Lau, A., & Takeuchi, D. (2001). Cultural factors in help-seeking for child behavior problems: Value orientation, affective responding, and severity appraisals among Chinese-American parents. *Journal of Community Psychology, 29*(6), 675–692.

Law, M., King, S., Stewart, D., & King, G. (2001). The perceived effects of parent-led support groups for parents of children with disabilities. *Physical and Occupational Therapy in Pediatrics, 21*(2–3), 29–48.

Lichtenstein, D., Lindstrom, L., & Povenmire-Kirk, T. (2008). Promoting multicultural competence: Diversity training for transition professionals. *The Journal for Vocational Special Needs Education, 30*(3), 3–15.

Losen, D. J., & Orfield, G. (Eds.). (2002). *Racial inequality in special education*. Cambridge, MA: Harvard Educational Publication Group.

Martin, N. (2009). *Arab American parents' attitudes toward their children's heritage language maintenance and language practices* (Master's thesis). Retrieved from ProQuest Dissertations and Theses database. (UMI No. 1472860).

Miles, M. (2007). *Islam, disability and deafness: A modern and historical bibliography, with introduction and annotation.* Retrieved from www.abdn.ac.uk/cshad/documents/ISLAM-DISAB-BibAbdn-070723.pdf

Moosa, S., Karabenick, S., & Adams, L. (2001). Teacher perceptions of Arab parent involvement in elementary schools. *School Community Journal, 11*(2), 7–26.

Moradi, B., & Hasan, N. T. (2004). Arab American persons' reported experiences of discrimination and mental health: The mediating role of personal control. *Journal of Counseling Psychology, 51*(4), 418–428.

Nagata, K. K. (2007). *The scale of attitudes towards disabled persons (SADP): Cross-cultural validation in a middle income Arab country, Jordan.* Retrieved from www.rds.hawaii.edu/ojs/index.php/journal/article/view/275/855

Nassar-McMillan, S., & Hakim-Larson, J. (2003). Counseling considerations among Arab Americans. *Journal of Counseling and Development, 81*(2), 150–159.

National Center on Secondary Education and Transition. (2004). *Current challenges facing the future of secondary education and transition services for youth with disabilities in the United States.* Retrieved from www.ncset.org/publications/discussionpaper

National Joint Committee on Learning Disabilities. (2005). *Responsiveness to intervention and learning disabilities.* Retrieved from www.asha.org/policy/TR2005–00303/

Nobles, A. Y., & Sciarra, D. T. (2000). Cultural determinants in the treatment of Arab Americans: A primer for mainstream therapists. *American Journal of Orthopsychiatry, 70*(2), 182–191.

Nydell, M. X. (1987). *Understanding Arabs: A guide for Westerners.* Bangor, ME: Intercultural Press.

Organization of the Islamic Countries. (2004). *Covenant on the rights of the child in Islam.* Retrieved from www.refworld.org/docid/44eaf0e4a.html

Palmer, B. C., El-Ashry, F., Leclere, J. T., & Chang, S. (2007). Learning from Abdallah: A case study of an Arabic-speaking child in a U.S. school. *The Reading Teacher, 61*(1), 8–17.

Parrish, T. (2002). Racial disparities in the identification, funding, and provision of special education. In D. J. Losen & G. Orfield (Eds.), *Racial inequity in special education* (pp. 15–37). Cambridge, MA: Harvard Education Press.

Phillips, E. (2008). When parents aren't enough: External advocacy in special education. *Yale Law Journal, 117*, 1802–1853.

Read, J. G. (2003). The sources of gender role attitudes among Christian and Muslim Arab-American women. *Sociology of Religion, 64*(2), 207–222.

Reiter, S., Mar'i, R. S., & Rosenberg, Y. (1986). Parental attitudes toward the developmentally disabled among Arab communities in Israel: A cross-cultural study. *International Journal of Rehabilitation Research, 9*(4), 355–362.

Samson, J. F., & Collins, B. A. (2012). *Preparing all teachers to meet the needs of English language learners.* Retrieved from files.eric.ed.gov/fulltext/ED535608.pdf

Sayed, M. A. (2003). Psychotherapy of Arab patients in the West: Uniqueness, empathy, and "otherness". *American Journal of Psychotherapy, 57*(4), 445–459.

Schwartz, W. (1999). Arab American students in public schools. *ERIC Digests* (ED 429144). Retrieved from http://iume.tc.columbia.edu/i/a/document/15693_Digest_142.pdf

Skiba, R. J., Simmons, A. B., Ritter, S., Gibb, A. C., Rausch, M. K., & Cuadrado, J. (2008). Achieving equity in special education: History, status, and current challenges. *Exceptional Children, 74*(3), 264–288.

Suleiman, M. W. (1999). *Arabs in America: Building a new future.* Philadelphia, PA: Temple University Press.

Tabbah, R. (2011). *Self-concept in Arab American adolescents: Implications of social support and experiences in the schools* (Doctoral dissertation). Retrieved from rave.ohiolink.edu/etdc/view?acc_num=osu1303938887

Taneije, S. (1998). *Arabic parents' involvement in American schools* (Master's thesis). Retrieved http://dc.library.okstate.edu/cdm/singleitem/collection/theses/id/421/rec/1

Thorp, E. K. (1997). Increasing opportunities for partnership with culturally and linguistically diverse families. *Intervention in School and Clinic, 32*(5), 261–269.

Trent, S. C., Kea, C. D., & Oh, K. (2008). Preparing preservice educators for cultural diversity: How far have we come? *Exceptional Children, 74*(3), 328–350.

Turmusani, M. (2003). *Disabled people and economic needs in the developing world: A political perspective from Jordan.* Hampshire, UK: Ashgate.

Turnbull, A. P., & Turnbull, H. R. (2001). *Families, professionals, and exceptionality: Collaborating for empowerment* (4th ed.). Upper Saddle River, NJ: Prentice-Hall.

U.S. Commission on Civil Rights. (2009). *Minorities in special education.* Washington, DC. Retrieved from www.usccr.gov/pubs/MinoritiesinSpecialEducation.pdf

Valles, E. C. (1998). The disproportionate representation of minority students in special education. *The Journal of Special Education, 32,* 52–54.

Vang, C. T. (2010). *An educational psychology of methods in multicultural education.* New York, NY: Peter Lang.

Villegas, A. M., & Irvine, J. J. (2010). Diversifying the teaching force: An examination of major arguments. *Urban Review, 42,* 175–192.

Warger, C., & Burnette. J. (2000). Reducing overrepresentation of diverse students. *ERIC Digest* #E596. Retrieved from www.teachervision.com/bilingual-education/teaching-methods/6049.html

Watanabe, M. (2006). *A cross-cultural comparison of attitudes toward persons with disabilities: College students in Japan and the United States* (Master's thesis). Retrieved from http://scholarspace.manoa.hawaii.edu/bitstream/handle/10125/6937/uhm005Fmed005F521005Fr.pdf?sequence=2

Westbrook, M., Legge, V., & Pennay, M. (1993). Attitudes towards disabilities in a multicultural society. *Social Science & Medicine, 36*(5), 615–623.

Zaromatidis, K., Papadaki, A., & Glide, A. (1999). A cross-cultural comparison of attitudes toward persons with disabilities: Greeks and Greek-Americans. *Psychological Reports, 84,* 1189–1196.

Zhang, D., & Katsiyannis, A. (2002). Minority representation in special education. *Remedial & Special Education, 23*(3), 180–187.

Further Readings

Adam, B. (2012). *How to provide culturally sensitive care to Arab American patients.* Retrieved from www.currentpsychiatry.com/article_pages.asp?AID=10928

Anees, S. (2006). Service delivery to an Arab and south Asian population. *International Journal of Diversity in Organizations, Communities and Nations, 8*(3), 59–64.

Balcazar, F., Dimpfl, S., Schiff, R., Suarez-Balcazar, Y., Taylor-Ritzler, T., & Willis, C. (2008). Cultural competence training with organizations serving people with disabilities from diverse cultural backgrounds. *Journal of Vocational Rehabilitation, 29*(2), 77–91.

Budman, C. L., Lipson, J. G., & Meleis, A. I. (1992). The cultural consultant in mental health care: The case of an Arab adolescent. *American Journal of Orthopsychiatry, 62*(3), 359–370.

Choi, K. H., & Wynne, M. E. (2000). Providing services to Asian Americans with developmental disabilities and their families: Mainstream service providers' perspective. *Community Mental Health Journal, 36*(6), 589–95.

Esposito, J. L. (2002). *What everyone needs to know about Islam.* New York, NY: Oxford University Press.

Lind, M. (2006). *Arab-Americans and the social worker: Cultural competence.* Retrieved from searchwarp.com/swa65808.htm

Meleis, A., & La Fever, C. (1984). The Arab American and psychiatric care. *Perspectives in Psychiatric Care, 12*(2), 72–86.

Ovando, C. J., Collier, V. P., & Combs, M. C. (2006). *Bilingual and ESL classrooms teaching in multicultural contexts* (4th ed.). Boston, MA: McGraw Hill.

Saleh, S. M., & Baqutayan, S. M. (2012). What is the Islamic society? *International Review of Social Sciences and Humanities, 2*(2), 113–119.

Salimbene, S. (2000). Providing culture-sensitive healthcare to people from the Middle East. In S. Salimbene (Ed.), *What language does your patient hurt in? A practical guide to culturally competent patient care.* (pp. 37–53). St. Paul, MN: EMC Paradigm.

Zahr, L. K., & Hattar-Pollara, M. (1998). Nursing care of Arab children: Consideration of cultural factors. *Journal of Pediatric Nursing, 13*(6), 349–355.

5 Conclusions

This chapter emphasizes the need for obtaining accurate information about the size, characteristics, and special circumstances of Arab American children with disabilities and their families. The chapter also encourages researchers to conduct research on this ethnic minority in the United States. Finally, the chapter calls upon teachers and service providers to gain familiarity with Arab American culture and move beyond commonly held beliefs and assumptions about Arabs.

If racial and ethnic minority children with disabilities in the United States have received little research attention, then Arab American children with disabilities have been almost totally ignored and forgotten. Because Arab Americans are not officially recognized as a minority group by the U.S. Office of Management and Budget, they are not listed as a separate ethnic group in disability databases. However, given that the U.S. Census figures on Arab Americans are widely believed to considerably underestimate the size of this population (Samhan, n.d.), estimating Arab Americans with disabilities based on these figures will likely be an undercount. Understandably, Arab American children with disabilities have been excluded from the literature pertaining to ethnic and minority students in special education and from surveys of disability prevalence estimates in the United States. Likewise, Arab American children with disabilities have been excluded from works published by both Arab American and non-Arab American writers and researchers. The glaring paucity of published literature pertaining to these children has been emphasized throughout this book. Relative to research on other U.S. ethnic and linguistic minority children with disabilities, research on disability among members of this population is in its infancy. The only empirical data available about the experiences of Arab American children and their families with the special education system in the United States are those presented in the three studies introduced in Chapter 2 (Abadeh, 2006; Donovan, 2013; Kuaider, 2005). Two of these studies were qualitative and included relatively very few conveniently selected participants (Donovan,

2013; Kuaider, 2005), and the third study (Abadeh, 2006) was quantitative and included a relatively large probability sample. The author's intention here was not to judge the scientific merit of these studies: all of them provide very enlightening and long-awaited data. Instead, the intent here was to emphasize the need for further research on Arab American children living with disabilities.

Without adequate information on the Arab American community, one is left basically with very little information regarding the size, characteristics, and needs of this invisible subminority of Arab American children with disabilities. Because of this scarcity in information on Arab Americans, the author has attempted to assemble as much data as possible and has made educated guesses based on them. To analyze important issues related to Arab American children with disabilities, the book provided (a) background information about the Arab American community, (b) a description of the current status of disability and special education in Arab countries, (c) a comprehensive review and synthesis of pertinent literature, (d) a discussion of methods Arab Americans can use to navigate the U.S. special education system, and (e) guidelines for culturally appropriate special education practices with Arab Americans. The author has made it clear that like other racial and other minority populations with disabilities in the United States, Arab Americans with disabilities and their families are likely to face various challenges. The Advisory Committee on Minority Health (2011) stated that "minorities with disabilities experience additional disparities in health, prejudice, discrimination, economic barriers, and difficulties accessing care as a result of their disability" (p. 11). In fact, Arab American students in U.S. schools may face more challenges than other minority students. These challenges result especially from negative stereotyping, racism and discrimination, and widespread misinformation about their history and culture through media, curriculum content, peer groups, and teachers (Haddad, 2004; Jackson, 1997; Schwartz, 1999; Suleiman, 1999; Yahya, 2010). Surveys of Arab American youth suggest a high prevalence of behavioral and psychological problems (Sulaiman, 2008). These problems have been attributed to the tension induced by acculturative stress especially among recent Arab Americans who are Muslim, negative perceptions and acts of violence toward the Arab American community, which may pose an additional stress to its members (Goforth, 2011). A child's disability, however, can cause additional stress for Arab American families. The lack of available research or resources on Arab American students causes difficulty for teachers trying to develop the skills and knowledge necessary for working with these students and their families (Goforth, 2011).

Special education literature emphasizes that problems may arise from service providers' lack of knowledge of cultural values and perspectives on children of diverse cultural, linguistic, ethnic, or religious backgrounds (Dunst, 2002; Martin, 2009; Ovando, Collier, & Combs, 2006; Terry & Irving, 2010). Prominent among these problems are disproportionate assignment to special education and low-quality instructional programs and practices (Gay, 2002; Terry & Irving, 2010). In contrast, effective parent involvement and parent–teacher relationships in the special education process can be useful to children, teachers, and parents. Thus, service providers should gain familiarity with Arab American children's culture, language, and perceptions, and move beyond commonly held beliefs and assumptions about Arabs so they can understand and support these children and their parents better and communicate more effectively and clearly with them. The author hopes that this book will provide a basis for further investigation of the unique needs and the challenges faced by Arab American children with disabilities and their families that would enable service providers to offer culturally and linguistically appropriate special education and related services for this population.

Given that knowledge about Arab Americans with disabilities is very scant, both quantitative and qualitative studies on this subminority in the United States are warranted. A wide variety of potential research topics exists relevant to disabilities among Arab Americans. These research topics include, but are not limited to, barriers to quality special education services and programs to Arab American children with disabilities, Arab Americans parents' knowledge of their rights and responsibilities and their children's rights, special education teachers' perceptions regarding their experiences teaching Arab American children with disabilities, and quality of life of Arab American families having children with disabilities. Future research exploring differences and similarities in disability among Arab Americans and other racial and ethnic minorities (e.g., African Americans, Asian Americans, Latin Americans) in the United States will also be helpful. Numerous benefits will accrue to teachers as well as policy makers and researchers from cross-cultural research examining the variation in how cultures interpret disability. Because very little is known about the prevalence of disabilities among Arab Americans, studies addressing this issue are needed. Studies similar in methodology to the one conducted by Dallo, Al Snih, and Ajrouch (2009) will be enlightening; however, such studies should cover different age levels and degrees of disability.

A need also exists for developing strategies to reach out to Arab American children with disabilities and promote cultural competency among service providers working with this population. The Advisory Committee on Minority Health (2011) recommended implementing the following procedures to address and overcome the lack of data, knowledge, and culturally competent care specific to minorities with disabilities: (a) raising awareness about minorities with disabilities at the federal, state, and local levels; (b) increasing the cultural competency of service providers in providing effective care and treatment for minorities with disabilities; (c) improving research and practice on disabilities in minority populations; and (d) strengthening the health care workforce to ensure appropriate, high-quality, and culturally competent care for people with disabilities. This book, despite cautioning against overgeneralizations about Arab American culture and family, contains some important characteristics of this population that can be helpful in this regard.

Special education and related service providers have increasing numbers of opportunities to work with culturally and racially diverse populations. The importance of culturally appropriate approaches with racially and linguistic diverse persons with disabilities and their families has been emphasized in recent years (Lichtenstein, Lindstrom, & Povenmire-Kirk, 2008; National Center on Secondary Education and Transition, 2004). Consistent with this approach, this book provided an overview of some culturally relevant information on Arab Americans with disabilities and their families, whose numbers have steadily increased in recent years.

- Lack of information and awareness may pose difficulties for both Arab Americans with disabilities and human service practitioners delivering services to them. This author implied that when working with Arab Americans with disabilities and their families, particularly those not acculturated to the American way of life, understanding issues related to acculturation, experiences in native countries, cultural influences on perceptions of disability, and traditional cultural expectations for the roles of the various family members can be especially useful for special education and related service providers. Overgeneralizations based on the information provided in this book, however, should be avoided. As noted previously, Americans of Arab descent constitute a heterogeneous group; they do not share the same traditions, beliefs, and practices. Thus, special education and related service providers should apply the information presented in this book with discretion while being mindful of the tremendous diversity of this population.
- Because perceptions of individuals with disabilities vary by culture, it is important that special education and related service providers working with Arab Americans develop an understanding of this population's cultural characteristics and practices. If culturally specific patterns of Arab American persons with disabilities and their families remain unidentified or misunderstood, then service providers' ability to offer appropriate programs for them will be undermined; and the challenges faced by these persons will increase.

- Perceptions of family honor, shame, and moral responsibility may lead families in collectivist societies, such as Arab societies, to hide family members with disabilities. The stigma attached to disability in the Arab region might lead some Arab American families to refuse disability-related services. Arab Americans, like many other ethnic minorities, may also be less likely to seek disability-related services because of factors such as language barriers, cultural and religious beliefs about special education and disabilities, gender role limitations, levels of acculturation, differences in social class, differing perceptions of disability, lack of bilingual service providers and culture-fair assessment tools, and perceived discrimination and negative stereotyping. Accordingly, extensive work with Arab American families may be particularly important during initial stages of referral and assessment. In addition, including the family in all decisions will be important to help family members feel that their honor is maintained and to promote acceptability of the assessment and programming.

- Arab Americans may find the system of special education and related services in the United States complicated and confusing. Due to several barriers (e.g., language difficulties, viewing the school as the authority, parents' previous experiences with service providers in native countries), intensive guidance and training are of critical importance when working with these families.

- Because Arab Americans frequently encounter negative stereotypes and perceptions, services offered for this population can be compromised. Special education and related service providers must ensure that Arab American persons with disabilities and their families are treated equitably and without prejudice. They must overcome their own prejudices, misconceptions, and knowledge gaps.

- As a result of cultural influences, many Arab American families tend to hide disability and would seek professional help only as a last resort. Special education and related service providers need to appreciate that disability can be stigmatizing and dehumanizing to the family in Arab culture. They also need to think of methods to overcome obstacles they may encounter as a result of this stigma and to overemphasize the confidentiality of information regarding the person and his or her family because of the sense of shame related to disability.

- Religion is of central importance to Christian and Muslim Arab Americans. Accordingly, consideration should be given to religious persuasion, but without stereotyping or assumptions.

- Many Arab Americans practice unique verbal and nonverbal communication styles and patterns. Some may face language barriers. Accordingly, special education and related service providers are better equipped to help Arab American persons with disabilities and their families if they attend to issues related to communication styles and patterns.

- Significant differences occur in acculturation among Arab Americans. Special education and related service providers must assess the level of acculturation of Arab American individuals and modify their style and intervention accordingly.

- Finally, a point emphasized repeatedly through this book is that very little information is available about Arab Americans with disabilities and their families. This dearth of data has impeded understanding of the unique needs of this minority. Overcoming this barrier could have advantages not only for Arab Americans with disabilities and their families, but also to special education and related service providers, researchers, and policy makers. In this era of evidence-informed decision making and practice, empirical studies on the unique needs of Arab Americans with disabilities are absolutely and obviously needed. Research-based data on various disability issues pertinent to Arab Americans would likely lead to a better understanding of the needs and characteristics of Arab American children with disabilities and their families. Furthermore, these data can contribute to the development of culturally appropriate assessment instruments and services as well as allocations of adequate funding.

References

Abadeh, H. (2006). *Perceptions of Arab American parents with children with special needs regarding home–school communications* (Doctoral dissertation). Retrieved from ProQuest Dissertations and Theses database. (UMI No. 304972765).

Advisory Committee on Minority Health. (2011). *Assuring health equity for minority persons with disabilities: A statement of principles and recommendations*. Retrieved from www.qualitymall.org/products/prod2.asp?prodid=30219

Dallo, F. J., Al Snih, S., & Ajrouch, K. J. (2009). Prevalence of disability among US and foreign-born Arab Americans: Results from the 2000 US Census. *Gerontology, 55*(2), 153–161.

Donovan, E. (2013). *A phenomenological exploration of Arab American parents' experiences with the special education process* (Doctoral dissertation). Retrieved from https://etd.ohiolink.edu/ap:0:0:APPLICATION_PROCESS=DOWNLOAD_ETD_SUB_DOC_ACCNUM:::F1501_ID:kent1372583897,inline

Dunst, C. J. (2002). Family-centered practices: Birth through high school. *Journal of Special Education, 36*(3), 139–147.

Goforth, A. N. (2011). Considerations for school psychologists working with Arab American children and families. *NASP Communique, 39*(6). Retrieved from www.nasponline.org/publications/cq/39/6/Multicultural-Affairs.aspx

Haddad, Y. Y. (2004). *Not quite American? The shaping of Arab and Muslim identity in the United States*. Waco, TX: Baylor University Press.

Jackson, M. L. (1997). Counseling Arab Americans. In C. C. Lee (Ed.), *Multicultural issues in counseling* (2nd ed., pp. 333–352). Alexandria, VA: American Counseling Association.

Kuaider, S. M. (2005). *Ecocultural study of Arab American families of children with disabilities* (Master's thesis). Long Beach, CA: California State University.

Lichtenstein, D., Lindstrom, L., & Povenmire-Kirk, T. (2008). Promoting multicultural competence: Diversity training for transition professionals. *The Journal for Vocational Special Needs Education, 30*(3), 3–15.

Martin, N. (2009). *Arab American parents' attitudes toward their children's heritage language maintenance and language practices* (Master's thesis). Retrieved from ProQuest Dissertations and Theses database. (UMI No. 1472860).

National Center on Secondary Education and Transition. (2004). *Current challenges facing the future of secondary education and transition services for youth with disabilities in the United States*. Retrieved from www.ncset.org/publications/discussionpaper

Ovando, C. J., Collier, V. P., & Combs, M. C. (2006). *Bilingual and ESL classrooms teaching in multicultural contexts* (4th ed.). Boston, MA: McGraw Hill.

Samhan, H. (n.d.). *By the numbers*. Allied Media Corp. Retrieved from www.allied-media.com/Arab-American/Arab_demographics.htm

Schwartz, W. (1999). Arab American students in public schools. *ERIC Digests* (ED 429144). Retrieved from http://iume.tc.columbia.edu/i/a/document/15693_Digest_142.pdf

Sulaiman, M. (2008). Mental health issues of Arab American youth. Paper presented at the *American Experience: A National Summit to Promote the Well-being of Arab and Muslim Youth*, Dearborn, MI.

Suleiman, M. W. (1999). *Arabs in America: Building a new future*. Philadelphia, PA: Temple University Press.

Terry, N. P., & Irving, M. A. (2010). Cultural and linguistic diversity: Issues in education. In C. M. O'Brouke & R. P. Colarusso (Eds.), *Special education for all teachers* (5th ed., pp. 110–132). Dubuque, IA: Kendall Hunt Publishing.

Yahya, H. A. (2010). *Arab American students in USA schools*. Retrieved from www.articlesbase.com/. . ./arab-american-students-in-usa

Index

acculturation 11–12, 86–7, 102; *see also* Arab culture
ADHD (attention-deficit/hyperactivity disorder) 25, 32, 33
adjustment disorders 33
Advisory Committee on Minority Health 98, 99
Advocates for Justice and Education 63
African cultures, attitude toward disabilities 45
alcohol consumption 8, 19
allied health sciences 49
ambulatory difficulty 27
American Community Survey (ACS) 5
American Sign Language (ASL) 31
American-Arab Anti-Discrimination Committee (ADC) 1, 13, 88
Americans with Disabilities Act 53
amputations 30
anxiety 11, 33, 36
anxiety disorder 33
Arab America Michigan 13
Arab American Association of New York (AAANY) 88
Arab American Center for Economic and Social Services 13
Arab American Chamber of Commerce 13
Arab American children: disproportionate identification of 74, 99; gendered expectations for 17; *see also* children with difficulties
Arab American culture *see* Arab culture
Arab American Family Services (AAFS) 88
Arab American Institute (AAI) 5, 13, 88

Arab American National Museum (AANM) 13, 88
Arab American National Museum 13
Arab American parents *see* families; fathers; mothers; parents
Arab Americans: acculturation of 11–12, 86–7, 102; adverse birth outcomes among 9; demographics 1–2, 4–6; diversity among 2–3; educational attainment and school experiences 6–7; family and culture 15–19; health status 8–9; language of 9–10; myths and facts about 14; perception of family 101; religious affiliation of 9; values of 15–16; work and income 8
Arab Americans with disabilities 50–3; advocacy for 87–8; estimated number of 25–8, 97; as overlooked subminority 24–5
Arab Community Center for Economic and Social Services (ACCESS) 88
Arab countries 1–2; assistive technology (AT) in 48; definition of disability in 40–1; human development in 2; perceptions of disability in 38–40; prevalence of disability in 41–3; special education and related services 46–50; women with disabilities in 45; *see also* challenges in Arab countries
Arab culture 15–19, 78, 81; awareness of 74; communication styles 10, 17, 75, 101–2; diet 18–19; dress 10, 18; and education 70; and family 75–6; as high-contact 17; perceptions of

disability in 38–40, 75; *see also* acculturation
Arab families *see* families
Arab human development report 2
Arabic Braille 32
Arabic language 9–10, 82–3
Arab immigration to the United States 4, 6
Arab–Israeli War 4
Arab Population: 2000 5
Arabs, media depictions of 12, 14; *see also* Arab Americans
Arab Spring 2, 39
armed conflicts 26, 44
Asian cultures, attitude toward disabilities 46
assessment: of Arab American children 74; of English language proficiency 78; for IDEA 61–2, 78; multicultural 65, 66
assistive technology (AT) 48
Assistive Technology Makes Independence Accessible (ATMIA) 51
AT (assistive technology) 48
ATMIA (Assistive Technology Makes Independence Accessible) 51
attention-deficit/hyperactivity disorder (ADHD) 25, 32, 33
autism 28, 29, 48, 61, 87–8
autism spectrum disorder 29
automobile accidents 44

Bandak, Lily 50–1
Bandak Foundation 50–1
behavior disorders 33, 47
behavior management issues 64
beliefs/historical perspectives, multicultural 66
Berber language 10
black and minority ethnic groups, in London 46
blindness 31–2, 41, 43, 47, 52, 53, 61; *see also* low vision; visual impairment
Blue Hands United of Dearborn 88
bronchial asthma 30

cancer 8, 30
cardiovascular disease 8, 9, 43, 44

Carroll Center for the Blind 52
CBR (community-based rehabilitation) 50
Center for Parent Information and Resources 63
cerebral palsy 30, 51
challenges in Arab countries: availability and adequacy of services 48; gap between policy and practice 48; lack of access to services 47–8, 49
charity work 47
children with difficulties: negative attitudes toward 45–6; rights of 62, 63, 87, 99; *see also* minority children with disabilities
Christian Arabs 4, 9, 11, 19, 85, 101
chronic diseases 9, 30, 44
chronic obstructive pulmonary disease 30
chronic respiratory conditions 44
Classical Arabic 9
clothing 10, 18
cognitive difficulty 27; *see also* intellectual disabilities (impairments)
colleges, undergraduate programs (degree) 48
Commission on Rehabilitation Certification 65
communicable diseases 44
communication, home–school 36, 37
communication skills, multicultural 66
communication styles 10, 17, 75, 101–2
community-based rehabilitation (CBR) 50
conduct disorders 33
confidentiality 63, 75–6
Connecticut Administrators of Programs for English Language Learners (CAPELL) 82
Council for Exceptional Children (CEC) 65
counselors 85
Cradle of Comedy (television series) 51
culture *see* acculturation; African cultures; Arab culture; Asian cultures

dating 17
deaf-blindness 28, 61
deafness 28, 41, 47, 61; *see also* hearing impairment

decision making, shared 62
degree programs 48
depression 11, 33, 86
depressive disorder 33
Detroit Arab American study 24, 82
developmental delay 28
diabetes 8, 9, 30, 43
diagnostic services 47
disability and disabilities: in Arab
    culture 38–40; in Asian cultures 46;
    attitudes regarding 76–7; categories of
    41; causes of 43–4; congenital factors
    43; defined 26, 40–1; estimated
    number of Arab Americans 25–8, 97;
    estimated numbers of people in Arab
    countries 42–3; examples of Arab
    Americans with 50–3; genetic factors
    43–4; IDEA categories of 28, 61; and
    marriage prospects 36–7; parents'
    denial of 68; prevalence of in Arab
    countries 26, 41–2; risk factors for 43;
    stigma associated with 30–2, 34–5,
    40, 41, 45–6, 64, 68–9, 75–8, 101;
    types of 27
discrimination 3, 4, 8, 45, 64, 68, 77,
    80, 86, 98, 101
diseases: chronic 9, 30, 44;
    communicable 44; genetic 43
double burden 64
double discrimination 64
Dow, Rabih 52
Down syndrome 43
dress, traditional 10, 18
drug abuse 9

economic disadvantage 64; *see also*
    poverty
Economic and Social Commission for
    Western Asia 49
education: in Arab countries 6, 10,
    32; of Arab American children
    with disabilities 69–70; of Arab
    Americans 6; effect of cultural
    beliefs on 70; equal access to 63;
    parental involvement in 10, 35, 62,
    68–9, 74, 79–82; *see also* special
    education
Education of All Handicapped Children
    Act 63; *see also* Individuals with
    Disabilities Education Act (IDEA)

Egypt, undergraduate programs in 49
ELLs (English language learners) 63–4,
    83–4
emotional disturbances 28, 61
endocrine disorders 43
English, learning by Arab Americans
    10–11
English as a second language (ESL)
    11, 66
English language learners (ELLs) 63–4,
    83–4
English language proficiency 74, 78,
    82–4; lack of 29
ESL (English as a second language)
    11, 66
ethnic groups, minority 46, 48
evaluations 62–3
explosions 44

families: in Arab culture 115–19,
    101; attitudes toward disabilities
    33–5, 68, 75–6, 78, 101; of
    children with disabilities 33–7;
    counseling and guidance for 69;
    extended 15, 45; help-seeking
    behaviors of 77–8; importance of
    76–8; involvement in education
    79–82; large size of 43; support for
    75; support of 86; *see also* fathers;
    mothers; parents
Family Empowerment and Disability
    Council 79
family-professional partnerships 69
FAPE (free appropriate public
    education) 61, 63
Farhat, Khodr 52–3
fathers: advanced age of 43; attitudes
    towards children's disabilities 68, 78;
    gender role of 16; involvement of 35,
    80; *see also* families; parents
food 18–19
free appropriate public education
    (FAPE) 61, 63

gender: and disability stigma 45;
    gender boundaries 79; gender roles
    17, 19, 85
genetic diseases/disorders 43
Global Deaf Muslim (GDM) 30–1
guide horses 53

Halal meat 19
Hashemite University 49
hate crimes 12
health: and acculturation 86; risk
    factors among Arab Americans 8–9;
    studies of Arab Americans 24–5
health care, poor 26, 44
health impairments 29–30
hearing impairment 27–8, 30–1, 46–7,
    61; *see also* deafness
heart disease 43
HIV/AIDS 30
home–school relationship 66, 70;
    communication 36, 37
human rights, in Arab communities 39
hypertension 8

IDEA *see* Individuals with Disabilities
    Education Act
IEP (individualized education program)
    62–3, 69
illiteracy 26, 44
illness, chronic 9, 30, 44
ILO (International Labour
    Organization) 50
immunizations 44
independent educational evaluation
    (IEE) 63
independent living difficulty 27
individualized education program (IEP)
    62–3, 69
Individuals with Disabilities Education Act
    (IDEA) 28, 61, 84, 87, 99; assessment
    for 61–2, 78; on family involvement
    79–82; procedural safeguards in 63;
    requirement for IEP 62
injuries, work-related 44
instruction, multicultural 66–7
intellectual disabilities (impairments)
    28, 30, 32, 41–2, 46, 47; *see also*
    learning disabilities
intergender relations 17
Iran, special education in 65
Iranian Americans 64
Islam, and disability 85; *see also*
    Muslim Arabs

Jordan, undergraduate programs in 49
Jordan University of Science and
    Technology 49

kinship marriage 26, 30, 39, 43
Kurdish language 10

landmines 44
language 9–10, 75; Arabic 9–10, 82–3;
    dialects 10
language barriers 70
language impairment 28, 47, 61
learning differences 67
learning disabilities 25, 28–9, 47; specific
    28, 61; *see also* intellectual disabilities
learning environments *see* school
    environment
least restrictive environment (LRE) 61
Lebanese American Heritage Club 52
Literary Arabic 9
living conditions, poor 2, 39, 44
low birth weight 9
low self-esteem 86
low vision 31–2, 42; *see also* blindness;
    visual impairment
LRE (least restrictive environment) 61

mainstreaming, of special students 47,
    77–8
malaria 44
malnutrition 44
marriages: arranged 17; interfamily 26,
    30, 39, 43
measles 44
meningitis 30, 44
mental health problems 33, 68–9; aid
    for 77; cultural perceptions of 34–5
Middle East 1; *see also* Arab countries
mineral deficiencies 44
minority children with disabilities
    24–8, 68, 74, 83, 97–8; in special
    education 63–7; *see also* children
    with difficulties
Modern Standard Arabic 9–10
mothers: advanced age of 43;
    blamed for children's disabilities
    35; involvement at school 79;
    satisfaction with family relationships
    35, 37; *see also* families; parents;
    women
multicultural competencies 65, 66
multiple disabilities 28
multiple sclerosis 50–1
muscular dystrophy 43

musculoskeletal disorders 30, 43; *see also* physical disabilities
Muslim Arabs 9, 11, 85, 101
The Muslims are Coming! (film) 51
muteness 30
myths, about Arabs and Arab Americans 14

National Arab American Medical Association (NAAMA) 13, 88
National Council on Disability 77
NCLB (No Child Left Behind) legislation 63, 82
Network of Arab American Professionals (NAAP) 13, 88
neurological disorders 30
neuropsychiatric disorders 43
New York Arab American Comedy Festival 51
NGOs (nongovernmental organizations) 50
No Child Left Behind (NCLB) legislation 63, 82
nongovernmental organizations (NGOs) 50

Obeidallah, Dean 51
occupational safety 44
occupational therapy 49
online resources 13, 68, 88
oppositional defiant disorder 33
orthopedic impairment 28, 41; *see also* physical disabilities
orthotic centers 48
other health impairment 28, 61
otitis media 30, 44
outreach and awareness programs 74
overweight 8

paralysis 30
parental consent 63
parents: attitudes toward children's disabilities 33–5; barriers to use of special education 68–70; culture-specific concerns of 36–7; denial of disabilities by 68; involvement in children's education 10, 35, 62, 68–9, 74, 79–82; perceptions of special education system 35, 36–8; relationships with children's teachers

36, 37; rights and responsibilities of 62, 63, 66, 69, 70, 99; safeguards for 62–3, 78; and the special education system 67–8
Parent Training and Information (PTI) centers 88
phenylketonuria 43
physical disabilities 29–30, 41, 43, 47
physical therapy 49
placement decisions 62–3
polygamy 35
post-traumatic stress disorder (PTSD) 33
poverty 26, 44, 64
preterm birth 9
prior written notice 63
private sector facilities 47
professional development training programs 48
prosthetic centers 48
psychological distress 86
psychological problems 33
psychosocial problems 86
PTSD (post-traumatic stress disorder) 33
public awareness 48
public health 9
pulmonary diseases 43

Qatar Assistive Technology Center 48
Qur'an 85

race, and underachievement 64
racial and ethnic populations, disability among 24–8, 64, 68, 74, 83, 97–8
racial conflict 70
racism 7, 66, 98
Ramouni, Mona 53
referral services 47
refugees, from Syria 2–3
regional awareness 48
rehabilitation: counseling and services 49; institution-based 49–50
religion 9, 36, 85, 101; *see also* Christian Arabs; Islam; Muslim Arabs
Response to Intervention (RtI) 83–4
retinitis pigmentosa (RP) 52; *see also* blindness; visual impairment

rights: of children 62, 63, 87, 99; of individuals 80, 85; of individuals with disabilities 41, 47, 77; of parents 62, 63, 66, 69, 70, 81, 99
RtI (Response to Intervention) 83–4

safeguards, for parents and students 62–3, 78
school: as authority 69; communication with home 36, 37
school environment 67; least restrictive 61; multicultural instruction 66–7; supportive 7
school experiences of Arab Americans 6–7
segregated institutions 46–7, 65
self-care difficulty 27, 29
sex roles *see* gender
sickle cell disorders 30, 43
sign language 30–1
social isolation 46
social networks 35
social work 68
special education 76–9; in Arab countries 46–7; categories of 30; and cultural diversity 98–9; culturally appropriate 74, 100; family participation in 69; major challenges in Arab countries 47–8; and minority ethnic children with disabilities 63–7; private and volunteer sector facilities 47; programs at Arab universities 47; and related services 46–50; in resource rooms 47; in self-contained classes 47
special education system: Arab American parents and 67–8; barriers to use by Arab Americans 68–70; family attitudes toward 35, 36–8; in the United States 38, 61–3, 67–9, 79–83
specific learning disability 28, 61; *see also* learning disabilities
speech and language impairments/disorders 28, 47, 61
speech and language pathologists 28, 49
spina bifida 30
spinal cord injuries 30
stereotypes 86–7; negative 3, 6–7, 11, 12–14, 33, 98, 101

stigma, attached to disability 30–2, 34–5, 40, 41, 45–6, 64, 68–9, 75–8, 101
stress 11, 33, 75, 76, 86, 98
students: mainstreaming of 47, 64, 77–8; safeguards for 62–3, 78
Syrian civil war 2
Syrian refugees 2–3

teachers 85; and cultural respect 81; parents' relationships with 36, 37; special education 65
technical assistance 50
teleconferencing 79
terrorist attacks (9/11) 12
thalassemia 43
tobacco use 8
trachoma 44
traffic accidents 44
traumatic brain injury 28, 61
tribes, extended 45
tuberculosis 44
Turkey, special education in 65
Turkish Americans 64

U.N. Convention on the Rights of People with Disabilities 47
underidentification 83
unemployment 2
UNESCO 50
United States: Arab immigration to 4–6, 9; attitudes toward disabilities in 46; denigration of Arab people in 12; racial and ethnic minorities with disabilities in 24–8, 64, 68, 74, 83, 97–8; special education services in 38, 61–3, 67–9, 79–83
University of Jordan 49

values, of Arab Americans 15–16
visual impairment 27, 28, 31–2, 47, 52, 53, 61; *see also* blindness; low vision
vitamin deficiencies 44
vocational rehabilitation and training 49
volunteer sector facilities 47

websites 13; Parent Training and Information (PTI) centers 88; of states 68
WHO (World Health Organisation) 50, 64

women: convention of covering 14, 18; with disabilities 45; *see also* mothers
work-related injuries 44
World Bank 50
World Health Organisation (WHO) 50, 64

You Don't Mess with the Zohan (film) 51

Zayid, Maysoon 51–2
Zero Reject principle 62

Printed in the United States
by Baker & Taylor Publisher Services